To the Ends of the Earth

How the First Jewish Followers of Yeshua Transformed the Ancient World

ENDORSEMENTS

Join Jeff Seif on a guided tour through the Messianic Jewish communities of the ancient Mediterranean world . . . and discover that these are not just a few scattered and marginal groups, but the true heirs of Yeshua's own apostolic band, which became the foundation of the Yeshua movement around the world and through the ages.

– Rabbi Russ Resnik, Union of Messianic Jewish Congregations

Jeffrey Seif writes an intelligent, insightful, and up-to-date history of the first Messianic Jews, and their enduring influence on the life of the early church. Contemporary scholarship has radically revised our understanding of this topic. I highly recommend this work for both Christians and Messianic Jews. We can only understand who we are if we understand where we come from.

– Mark S. Kinzer, Ph.D.

Most Christians, even scholars, are virtually ignorant of the early Jewish Jesus believers of the ancient church. In a careful and scholarly treatment, Jeffrey Seif provides a helpful presentation of this important subject that is essential for understanding the gospel among the Jewish people.

– Michael Rydelnik, Ph.D., Professor of Jewish Studies, Moody Bible Institute, Author of The Messianic Hope: Is the Hebrew Bible Really Messianic?

I am glad to endorse Jeffrey Seif's new book. Jeffrey is a great writer who consistently provides both good scholarship and creative insight to the great benefit of the Church and the Messianic Jewish community. -- Dan Juster, Th.D.

Dr. Seif's book on early Messianic Jewish theology and practice is an important contribution to understanding the early Church and its development. In our day, God is restoring a "first-century perspective" on how the early believers lived and thought. I wholeheartedly recommend this book.

– Wayne Wilks Jr., Ph.D., International Director, Messianic Jewish Bible Institute

Dr. Seif's book promises to give the inside scoop on the world-changing Messianic movement of the first century. It's history worth knowing as the world reconsiders who the original Yeshua and his earliest followers really were.

– Rabbi Glenn David Blank, Ph.D., Beit Simcha Congregation, Literary Editor of the Tree of Life Bible

Seif adds his voice to the growing chorus of scholars arguing for a centuries-old Jewish-friendly Messianic Judaism. It can now be seen that the Jewish foundations of a vibrant Messianic Jewish faith extend from Yeshua through the first century and well into the second century--throughout the whole of the Mediterranean world.

– Rabbi Jeffrey Feinberg, Ph.D.

Jeffrey Seif guides us through the story of "Christian" beginnings in the ancient Mediterranean world. Seif does some detective work in the process. He snoops around the ancient Greco-Roman world, gathers facts, builds a case, and presents it to the jury--his readers. Will his case be compelling enough to make you a believer in his thesis? Read the book with an open mind and find out!

– Jim Garlow, Ph.D., Senior Pastor, Skyline Church, San Diego, CA

Jeff Seif has written a book that is scholarly, engaging, and lively. Seif leads the reader on a fascinating journey into one of the least understood, mysterious, and yet central questions of the Church age: What exactly happened to the first believers of the age - the Jewish disciples, communities, teachers, and messengers of Messiah. The reader is taken on a quest into one of the most important and ancient of mysteries, but one that yields a multitude of surprising discoveries.

– Rabbi Jonathan Cahn, Beth Israel Congregation

Dr. Jeffrey Seif weaves a scholarly soliloquy about the Early New Testament and post-New Testament Messianic Jewish experience. Very few scholars have addressed this subject so dutifully. Seif meticulously details aspects of early Church history and begs the question: What really happened, and who were these people? Readers are going to find out, and many will be surprised in the process!

– Barri Mallin, Ph.D.

Dr. Jeffrey Seif's new book is a well-researched work that deftly investigates the long searched for "missing links" in Messianic Jewish history. This book is an absolute must for the libraries of every serious reader of early Christian-Jewish relations.

– Rabbi Michal Wolf, Beth Messianic Congregation, Cincinnati, Past President of the Messianic Jewish Alliance of America

"When did we forsake the Jewish roots of our faith in the Jewish Messiah and World Redeemer and become a new religion called "Christianity?" Jeffrey Seif gives convincing evidence that Jewish and Gentile believers in the early centuries were closely connected to each other and to the their Jewish roots, and less embracing of Roman pagan influences. Very helpful for those of us who embrace the profound Jewishness of the early believers!"

– Rev. Don Finto, "Raising up generations of Calebs and Joshuas"

Seif raises questions and offers answers as to the reasons for the rise and eventual dissolution of the early church as a vibrant Messianic Jewish community. Giving a voice to these first believers in their Jewish context, Seif explores who they were, how they effected history, and how their communities continue to impact us today. We begin to sense what the story felt like in its early days, and, where we may find ourselves in that very same story today. Five stars, hands down!

– Mark Anthony, M.Div., Equipping & Leadership | Gateway Church

To the Ends of the Earth

How the First Jewish Followers of Yeshua Transformed the Ancient World

By Dr. Jeffrey L. Seif

Lederer Books
A division of
Messianic Jewish Publishers
Clarksville, MD 21029

Scripture quotations are taken from the New King James Version.

2017 2
Library of Congress Control Number: 2012941581
ISBN: 9781936716463

Printed in the United States of America

Published by
Lederer Books
A division of
Messianic Jewish Publishers
6120 Day Long Lane
Clarksville, Maryland 21029
Distributed by
Messianic Jewish Resources Int'l.
www.messianicjewish.net
Individual and Trade Order line: 800-410-7367

Email: lederer@messianicjewish.net

Dedication

Few men alive are more dedicated to exploring and telling the Messianic Jewish story in all its facets. Through the miracle that is television, Ken Berg (of Berg Productions) has spoken to untold millions. This book is dedicated to him, my friend—a hero who has done more with his life to advance the Messianic Kingdom than most of us could ever even imagine.

Special Thanks

The book you have in hand started as a paper I presented at the Union of Messianic Jewish Congregations' in-service in the summer of 2011. I am indebted to Rabbi Russ Resnik for inviting me on behalf of the committee, and getting the ball rolling for this book as a result. While there, Rabbi Barry Rubin encouraged me to continue to roll the ball uphill, to expand the work and develop it into its present form. Further encouragement came when Rabbi Marty Waldman of Baruch HaShem Congregation, Dallas, asked me to teach an adult education class at the synagogue, where I used the expanding paper. The book's final form came after its use at one of the doctoral classes I taught at Kings University/Seminary in the fall of 2011. Lastly, the book was further tweaked when I used a form of it for an abbreviated Yeshiva I was asked to conduct for a regional conference in Cincinnati of the Messianic Jewish Alliance of America, held in November 2011.

In sum, the volume you have in hand made its rounds between professional Messianic rabbis and scholars at the UMJC's summer leadership in-service, as with those at the MJAA's regional in-service in the fall of 2011. Interested Messianic laity at one of the largest Messianic congregations in the world interacted with me and helped improve it, as did doctoral students in the course I taught for individuals securing a degree in Messianic Jewish studies at Kings University. I owe a debt of gratitude to all who gave me helpful feedback and encouragement.

In this process, the book also made its way into the able hands of M. Taylor, M.Ed., a librarian with the Dallas Theological Seminary; Linda LaBreche, M.A., a research assistant at Wycliffe Bible Translators; and José Aquire, a student and assistant of mine at CFNI, Dallas. They helped me develop and tidy it up a bit, and for that I am forever grateful.

This book focuses on the rise and demise of the very first Messianic communities. *It endeavors to get to, and speak for, the very first Jewish advocates for Yeshua's Messiahship in and beyond Israel.* In a world where others are more predisposed to separate Christians from Jews, accept the "parting of the ways," and alight upon Messianic Jews' alleged disregard for the ancient Jewish people and religion, I defend Messianic experience and challenge the legitimacy of the parting of the ways, arguing for connection and not disconnection all the while.

I may not have asked and answered all my questions perfectly, and will stand corrected by those more able. It is my hope that a generation of newer and younger Messianic scholars will develop competencies way beyond my own and, with their own unique enthusiasms, energies, and abilities, wrestle with the book's principal questions. If all I accomplish with this book is to raise issues and ideas to galvanize further inquiries by men and women younger and better than myself, I would indeed be pleased.

Jeffrey L. Seif
2011

Contents

Foreword xv

Introduction xvii

Chapter 1
Reassessing Christian History 1

Chapter 2
Jerusalem-Based Messianic Judaism 15

Chapter 3
The Demise of Jerusalem-Based
Messianic Judaism 25

Chapter 4
Jewish Influences in the Levantine
Culture and Congregations 43

Chapter 5
Pro-Judaic and Anti-Judaic Tendencies
in the Ancient Roman World 79

Chapter 6
Jewish and Christian Contacts and
Influences in Europe 97

Chapter 7
Jewish and Christian Contacts and
Influences in North Africa 119

Conclusion 147

About the Author 151

ROMAN IMPERIUM
(ROMAN EMPIRE)
OCEANUS ATLANTICUS
OCEANUS GERMANICUS
OCEANUS GALLICUS
HIBERNIA
BRITANIA
CALDONIA
CIMBRI
SAXONES
VANDA
GERMA
BATAVI
BELGE
BOIOHEMU
ALLEMANI
Danubius Fl.
GALLIA
RHAETIA
HISPANIA
Durius Fl.
Tagus Fl.
Anas Fl.
Iberius Flu.
Pyrenei Mons
Rhodanus F.
Placentia Padus Fl
ITALIA
CORSICA
SARDINIA
BALEARES
SICILIA
MARE
MAURETANIA
NUMIDIA
AFRICA
TRIPOLITANA
SYRT
LOTOPHAG
Sabus Vel Sisaus Fl.

SARMATIA
BUDINI
AESTII
SCYTHIA
HAMAXOBII
GELONI
BASTARNAE
RHOXOLANI ALANI
JAZYGES
SARMATIA ASIATICA
DACHIA
JAZYGES METANASTAE
TAURICA
PALUS MAEOTIS
PONTUS EUXINUS
THRACIA
MACEDONIA
PONTIUS
ARMENIA
IBERIA
GALATIA
ASIA MINOR
CAPPADOCIA
MESOPOTAMIA
PHRYGIA
LYDIA
CARIA
PAMPHYLIA
LYCIA
CYPRUS
CRETA
AEGUM MARE
MARE
TERRANEUM
PHOENICIA
JUDAEA
IDUMEA
ARABIA PETRAEA
ARABIA
CYRENAICA
MARMARICA
AEGYPTUS
LIBYA
NASAMONES
Rha Occidentalis
Turunthus Flu.
Rubo Flu.
Borysthenes Flu.
Tanais Flu.
Rha Flu.
Vistula Flu.
Carpatia Mons
Hypanis Flu.
Tyras Flu.
Ister Flu.
Olbia
Tyra
Napuca
Nicopolis
Sindica
Pityus
Dioscurias
Trapezus
Sinope
Carambis Pr.
Heraclea
Gordium
Iconium
Pergamus
Sardes
Miletus
Taurus M.
Tarsus
Hierapolis
Alexandria
Thapsacus
Palmyra
Edessa
Carrae
Euphrates Fl.
Tigris Fl.
Salamis
Paphos
Curias
Rhodus
Cydonia
Gnossus
Samonium Pr.
Tripolis
Sidon
Tyrus
Caesarea
Joppa
Gaza
Damascus
Philadelphia
Canopus
Alexandria
Memphis
Cynopolis
Ammon
Augila
Cyrene
Barca
Antipyrgus
Paraetonium
Tripolis
Petra
Larissa
Delphi
Zacynthus
Messene
Melos
Cythera
Perinthus
Philippi
Byzantium
Apollonia
Odessus
Tomi
Istri Ostia
Udon Fl.
Anticites Flu.
Caucasus Mons
Cyrus Fl.
Artaxata
Satala
Melitene
Nisibis
Resaena
Apamea
Antiochia

Foreword

When I began reading Dr. Seif's new book, I felt that I was being *let in* on a secret…that is the history of the founding and spread of Messianic Judaism in the first few centuries following the Messiah's death and resurrection. I felt as if I was reading a part of my own family history—a history that I thought had been forever lost in the fog of history.

What happened to Messianic Judaism in the centuries after Yeshua's death and resurrection? How did it spread to such a thoroughly pagan and non-Jewish world? How long did its Jewish expression last? Why did it disappear and when? How did faith in Yeshua (Jesus) become so non-Jewish?

Dr. Seif looks at all available historical materials that reference this important time period from the context and perspective of today's Messianic Jewish revival of which he is part, as he seeks to answer these questions. He wants us to understand Messianic Judaism in the way the Jewish Apostles viewed the spread of the Jewish gospel of Messiah's salvation to the then known world. Dr. Seif parts the veil of history and recreates a fascinating and unique picture of the growth of Messianic Judaism throughout the Roman Empire and beyond.

I love the way he develops this history! He starts in Jerusalem where Messianic Judaism was born and was headquartered, then moves to Antioch where the first major center for Messianic faith developed outside of Israel, works his way around the Mediterranean to Asia Minor, Greece, Rome, Spain, Carthage, and Cyrene in North Africa, as well as to Alexandria, Egypt. He describes the evolution of this prophetic Messianic and Jewish faith among Jews and Gentiles alike.

For me, one of the most transforming revelations about early Messianic Judaism is that it was spreading throughout the Roman Empire for at least 200 years after Israel proper had been destroyed in 136 C.E. and the Jewish people exiled from our own land. As Dr. Seif explains, the Messianic Jewish community of the first few hundred years was very prominent and influential in virtually every corner of the Roman Empire where there was a large Jewish community.

Like most scholars and students of history, I assumed that the Messianic Judaism of the Apostles essentially disappeared after the defeat of Israel's army by the Romans in the Bar Kochba revolt (132-136 C.E.) thus relegating Messianic Judaism to *a flash in the historic pan*. This *flash-in-the-pan* perspective has been used by both traditional Christian and Jewish scholars, to discredit and minimize the importance of the Jewishness of faith in Jesus. While there have been other books written about this time period as it relates to the spread of Messianic Judaism, or as it is known today in its non-Jewish clothing—Christianity, none have been written from such a Jewish and Messianic vantage point.

I believe that this fascinating and exciting book will be seen in the years to come as one of the most important and prophetic books that has emerged from the modern Messianic Jewish revival.

Joel Chernoff
General Secretary
Messianic Jewish Alliance of America (and formerly of Lamb)

Introduction

What became of the first Jewish followers of Yeshua (Jesus)? This book examines the origin of the Yeshua movement and sets the record straight about how the appeal of Judaism and the message of the Messiah combined to transform the ancient pagan world. Readers may be surprised and intrigued to discover that Torah-observant Jewish believers in Yeshua and Gentile believers were actually more in concert than in conflict. There is another story than the one commonly heard about what we call Christian beginnings. The notion that the early Jewish followers of Yeshua disdained Judaism and went on to start a new religion, happily divested themselves of their Jewish heritage as soon as possible, needs to be reassessed.

This book offers an in-depth exploration of the impact of these unified communities of Jewish and Gentile believers throughout the Mediterranean region in the periods now labeled as the Apostolic, sub-Apostolic, and post-Apostolic eras. The fact that Christian theology employs these terms for that period of time and assigns the dating of history as B.C. and A.D., will also be discussed later in this book. Please note that C.E. in this book refers to the "Common Era" (otherwise known as A.D.) and B.C.E. means "Before the Common Era" (otherwise termed B.C.).

Though they were not known by this name at the time, I use the term *Messianic* throughout this book to identify these early followers of Yeshua, even though many traditionally but mistakenly call them "early Christians." Readers will consider the forces that drove Messianic Jews out of their ancestral homeland after the movement's founding there and will follow their journeys through Antioch and Syria, then in and around major cities in Asia Minor, Greece, Italy, and Spain. Once we cover the rapid spread of the Messianic movement's European beginnings, the rise of Messianic Jewish communities in the prominent North African cities of Carthage, Cyrene, and Alexandria will then be addressed, briefly, through an assessment of the historical record.

As we journey through the ancient Mediterranean world, we will pay attention to Messianic voices from that world, along with Messianic-related circumstances transpiring within it. Assessments of historical biblical literature will be offered, as will appraisals from non-canonical literature that give a window into what the early movement was principally about. To assist in developing an informed perspective, special attention will be given to lifting ancient voices from the *Pseudepigrapha*, from the *Didache* and *Didascalia*, and from the *Clementine Recognitions*, to name but a few here. Translations of the ancient writings of Josephus, Eusebius, St. Augustine, St. Jerome, Epiphanius, Seneca, and Dio Cassius will be leaned upon to reconstruct Messianic experience just north of Israel, in and around a place called the Levant. Tertullian, Cyprian, and the perspectives of a host of ancient historians and commentators will be called upon to assist with reconstructions of Messianic experience in Asia Minor, Italy, and North Africa.

Reflections from a host of modern scholars providing astute analysis will be reported and considered. We will hear from a variety of biblical scholars, philologists, historians, sociologists, and all kinds of "ologists," in fact—women and men, Jews and Christians, liberals, conservatives, and secular-minded people alike. I hope that by means of it all, we might even hear something from the Lord—though as the presenter I can only humbly request that and not promise it.

That will be for you to judge—later.

CHAPTER 1

REASSESSING CHRISTIAN HISTORY

In the Gospels, an itinerant Messianic figure named Yeshua made his way through the Jewish world and drew Jewish people's attention to his person and message in the process. Though it seemed he was maliciously cut down in his prime, his death and burial were judged to bestow salvation and were given theological import by the Jewish authors who penned the New Testament to offer an accounting of his life and teachings. After his death and burial, his resurrection—an event that revitalized his dispirited followers—is reported in these writings. This news, coupled with a resulting Pentecost experience that set off an explosion of new energies, provided the impetus for a post-Yeshua signs-and-wonders movement. This movement kept his message and his memory alive—enabling his story to go global in the course of time.

Communities bearing Yeshua's name, memory, and message have offered various accountings of his character and culture, and their own, ever since the penning of the New Testament. Advocates speaking for various post-Yeshua Christian communities today tend to tell different stories of what it means to be authentically Christian. They also have different ways of authorizing their Christian storytellers to win the affection and support of their followers.

Catholic religious authorities, for example, base their claims on the belief that power was given to St. Peter, then literally handed down to clerics in their denomination. Unable to use the leverage from historical claims and "Apostolic succession," Protestants gain support by insisting that theirs is a pristine telling of the New Testament's story, one that has not been adulterated by centuries of ancient and medieval religious additions, and, as a result, is more in line with the Apostolic witness in the New Testament. They stake their claim on *accuracy* not *history.* In contrast to the historical tradition of the Catholics and the intellectual foundation of the Protestants, Pentecostals base their authorization on a belief that the Pentecostal *experience* is what connects them to the religion's primal impulses. They claim it moves their adherents closest to the intentions of the New Testament authors.

These Christian denominations each claim to be best connected to the first impulses of an Israel-based Messianic movement, do they not?[1] Each announces itself as the movement's best representative. Each offers its own reasons for its arguments.

The Roman Catholic Church garners support for its authority over the minds, hearts, and behavior of its followers through a doctrine called "Apostolic Succession." The idea of "succession" supports the position of the institution's magistrates over its subordinate constituents. Based on a supposed direct descent from the Christian religion's founders (i.e., the Apostles) and from the principal founder himself (Jesus Christ)—submitting to the church today is seen as on par with submitting to Jesus and the Apostles yesterday.

Later revisionist-minded protestors (what we call "*Protest*-ants" today), 1500 years removed from the original Christian inception and expansion, were unable to garner support for their positions by appeals to the Christian past—i.e., to *history*. Protestantism secured leverage over the hearts and minds of late medieval Christians on the basis of its *theology*—not on purported claims of the historical descent of its advocates. Protestant theological ideas were said to have descended directly from Yeshua himself and the Apostles, even though their institutions did not make this claim. Promoted by an invention called the printing press, the new ideas circulated among impressionable individuals—over and against the objections of the reigning Catholic Church. Believing that Protestant theologians possessed the real Christian understanding of the New Testament's

1. These distinctions and claims will be explained further in later chapters.

message and meaning, more and more people took a leap of faith into the developing Protestant worldview—believing that they could be real and authentic Christians even though they had no claim to be the first Christians, historically, as the Catholics did.

But what if they are all equally wrong? What if, theological differences aside, they all have in common a nearly complete ignorance and/or denial of the origin of the movement they claim to best represent? The book you have in hand is written with the belief that speaking of early "Christian" history or theology (refracted through either Catholic or Protestant lenses) is both misleading and counterproductive. Offered here is a more accurate, and thoroughly Jewish, approach to Christian history and theology. By exploring the Yeshua Movement's rise in first-century Judea and its advancement in the Mediterranean world of the second and third century, this book accentuates how the first adherents placed a premium on continuity with the ancestral Jewish religion that informed their worldviews there.

In support of this particular thesis, in *The Rise of Christianity: A Sociologist Reconsiders History* (Princeton University Press), Professor Rodney Stark argues that "Jewish Christianity"—as he refers to it—"played a central role until much later in the rise of Christianity" than has previously been granted. He goes on to speak of the Jews of the "diaspora," a term often employed to note Jews living outside Israel proper. According to Dr. Stark, it was the "Jews of the diaspora who provided the initial basis for church growth during the first and early second centuries," and that Jewish people "continued as a significant source of Christian converts"[2]—to use his language, again—"until at least as late as the fourth century." This may come as quite a surprise to many in Christian circles, as it is contrary to conventional wisdom. His perspective presses individuals to consider the essence and substance of early Christian experience, and place both more directly in the realm of Jewish experience. In agreement with Professor Stark, I take aim in this book at this time-honored misconstruction of the facts and argue that Messianic Judaism indeed lived on, as did the Jewish Yeshua-believing community.

The traditional view has long asserted that, soon after inception, Christianity (1) moved away from the Jewish people, (2) happily shed its unneeded and unwanted Jewish "baggage," and (3) "providentially" morphed into the non-Jewish religion that we know it to be today—Christianity.

In support of this particular time-honored and preferred thesis, in his acerbic book *Modern Jews Engage the New Testament*, Reformed Jewish rabbi Michael J. Cook, a professor at Hebrew Union College, posits that Jews were phased out immediately. He argues that the early Jewish-related "Jesus movement" morphed into a decidedly anti-Jewish, Gentile "Christian" institution, and discarded its Jewish contingency soon afterward. Rabbi Cook states emphatically that by "the time of the Gospels' completion (70–100 C.E.) most Christians were of Gentile and not Jewish extraction,"[3] thus the church was principally constituted by its "Gentile influx"

2. Rodney Stark, *The Rise of Christianity: A Sociologist Reconsiders History* (Princeton: Princeton University Press, 1996), p. 49.

3. Michael J. Cook, *Modern Jews Engage the New Testament: Enhancing Jewish Well-Being in a Christian Environment* (Woodstock: Jewish Lights Publishing, 2009), p. 12 and passim.

of new members, not Jews.[4] Though he notes that "Gentile-Christians... had co-existed relatively harmoniously...with Jewish-Christians clearly dominant during the early decades,"[5] he isn't mindful to tell that story or develop that harmony in the least, anxious as he is to prove to his satisfaction that the divide between Jews and Gentiles was both swift and decisive after but a few years.[6]

Speaking of Yeshua in his *The Sage from Galilee: Rediscovering Jesus' Genius*, the late Israeli Professor David Flusser of the Hebrew University, Jerusalem, seemed more gracious by nature and much more inclined to underscore connections between early Yeshua believers and Jews. "The founder of their religion was a Jew faithful to the law," said Dr. Flusser, with Yeshua "never shown in conflict with the current practice of the law."[7] In time, however, like Rabbi Cook, though Professor Flusser notes the connection between Yeshua's bond with the Torah and that of his disciples and the Torah, he says the connection morphed into *disconnection*: "the Gentile church was born, and Christianity's ties to Judaism began unraveling"[8] immediately thereafter.

4. Ibid., p. 195.

5. Italics mine; ibid., p. 203.

6. Rabbi Cook says the better part of those early Christians were Jewish traitors and Gentiles who "rejected the Law of Moses" and believed God "turned from Jews to Gentiles" (ibid., p. 78)—a prejudice modern Jews can neither understand or abide. (Ibid., p. 80) The infamous "Judas" Iscariot (spelled *Ioudas*) and the word for "Jew" (spelled *Ioudaios*) are intentionally similar, in his mind's eye, so as to facilitate the linking of the two in memory, further contributing toward the parting of the ways between Christians and Jews. (Ibid., p. 176). Elsewhere, on p. 197, he speaks of accentuating negatives about Jews and omitting positives.

7. David Flusser, *The Sage from Galilee: Rediscovering Jesus' Genius* (Grand Rapids: Eerdmans, 2007), p. 35.

8. Ibid., p. 163.

In *The Jewish Reclamation of Jesus: An Analysis & Critique of the Modern Jewish Study of Jesus*, Professor Donald Hagner of the Fuller Theological Seminary said, "Christianity itself is regarded as largely the creation of the Apostle Paul, who... brought a new religion into existence," one distinct from Judaism.[9] Dr. Hagner went on to note Paul is "too antithetical to Judaism to receive a very fair treatment at the hands of Jews."[10] "New religion"? "Distinct"? "Antithetical to Judaism"? Dr. Hagner then matter-of-factly spoke of a "Pauline antinomian perspective that had begun to dominate the church,"[11] along with it being "Jesus' purpose to annul rabbinic interpretations of the Law"[12] in the first place.

All this will be called into question in this book. Before doing so, and before rushing to credit Paul with the creation of this *anti*-Jewish Christianity, consider that though he is appropriately held to be the decisive authority for what it means to be a "Christian" today, in his own day and time, and for long after, Paul was *not* universally considered the absolute and final authority on all things Christian.

Writing in *The Jews in Late Ancient Rome: Evidence of Cultural Interaction in the Roman Diaspora*, Professor Leonard Victor Rutgers points out, "In the western part of the [ancient] Mediterranean [world] the letters of Paul initially failed to make a significant impression in Christian circles. Only in the second half of the fourth century C.E. did writers start to take his writings more seriously... [resulting]

9. Donald Hagner, *The Jewish Reclamation of Jesus: An Analysis & Critique of the Modern Jewish Study of Jesus* (Eugene: Wipf and Stock Publishers, 1997), p. 26.

10. Ibid., p. 67.

11. Ibid., p. 120.

12. Ibid., p. 132.

in the increase in the number of commentaries on the letters of Paul."[13] This is significant because, even if Paul was anti-Jewish (and he wasn't), the universal influence of his perspectives and authority at the time in question cannot be assumed, given that he did not wield the kind of influence in the ancient Christian world as he does in the modern one, nearly 2,000 years removed.

According to Dr. Rutgers, the interest in Paul's New Testament writings in late antiquity was actually furthered by "a question that had threatened to rip apart early Christian communities as they sprang up in various parts of the Mediterranean during the first century: To what extent is Mosaic Law incumbent upon non-Jews who believed that Jesus was the Messiah?"[14] According to Professor Rutgers, those who wanted to distance themselves and the Messianic movement from Jewish culture discovered Paul afresh, based on being able to make Paul their ally in their struggle against Judaism.

Commentators in late antiquity, like Marius Victorinus, alighted upon Paul's supposedly wanting to call people "back from Judaism." Ambrosiaster, for his part, argued that circumcision and dietary restrictions were not to be normative and were promulgated to "punish" Jews and, with Victorinus, that "Jewish religious practices had become superfluous" given that "Jews had ceased to be the people of God" and that their laws were little more than "things of the past." St. Jerome and St. Augustine are similarly cited in support of this understanding, since they gave popular credence to it.[15]

13. Leonard Victor Rutgers, *The Jews in Late Ancient Rome: Evidence of Cultural Interaction in the Roman Diaspora* (New York: E. J. Brill, 1995), p. 219.

14. Ibid., p. 228.

15. Ibid., pp. 228–233.

However, were Paul's writings antithetical to Judaism, as Professor Hagner would have us believe? Because, in all fairness to Dr. Hagner, he's simply parroting the perspective that has prevailed for years. Was Paul really *antinomian* (i.e., law-less), as the scholars have forever represented him to be since the earliest centuries of Christian history and memory? The conventional reckoning answers an emphatic "Yes!" This volume answers with a resounding "No!"

In his updated doctoral dissertation from Cambridge University in 2007, writing under the title *A Jew to the Jews: Jewish Contours of Pauline Flexibility in 1 Corinthians 9:19–23*, Dr. David J. Rudolph offers a dissenting opinion and postulates that "Paul [actually] promoted Jewish continuity in his congregations… [and] that [he believed] Jews were to remain practicing Jews in keeping with their calling."[16] How this was indeed so will be considered in greater detail below.

In response to Paul's statement in 1 Cor. 9:20, "though I myself am *not*[17] under the Law," a favorite verse to many, Rabbi Rudolph suggests that, rather than a universal abandonment of the Torah, Paul was referring to an element of its "Pharisaic" and "strict interpretation." Dr. Rudolph points out that Paul actually remained "a Pharisee in kinship, custom, and education," opting only to challenge some Pharisaic traditions associated with interactions with Gentiles, less-binding food laws, and other vehicles of social cohesiveness and intercourse.[18]

16. David J. Rudolph, *A Jew to the Jews: Jewish Contours of Pauline Flexibility in 1 Corinthians 9:19–23* (Tubingen: Mohr Siebeck, 2011), p. 212.

17. Italics mine.

18. Rudolph, *A Jew to the Jews*, p. 202.

In sum, claiming Paul as the source of all things anti-Jewish, Christians (as noted above) and Jews (as noted previously) have been eager to perpetuate the antinomian myth, thereby separating "orthodox" Christianity from its allegedly "unorthodox" Jewish matrix. Preferring to highlight the parting of the ways between Jews and Christians (and Paul's supposed encouragement of it), few have stopped to consider the *enduring effect* that Jewish culture actually had on early Christianity—well past the times granted by Professors Cook, Flusser, Hagner, and Rutgers.

Building upon Dr. Rudolph's pro-Jewish assessment of Paul, and Professor Stark's Jewish-friendly assessment of early, post-Pauline Christianity, I will press the point further and say that often-used and anachronistic terms like "Christianity" itself, "Jewish Christianity," or "Jewish conversion to Christianity" are all misleading. Along those lines, the employment of post-Jewish, Christianized historical terms like "Christian Era," "Apostolic Era," "Sub-Apostolic Era," and "Post-Apostolic Era"[19] similarly have misleading effects[20] that create obstructions to a clear understanding.

Specialists cannot help but create discipline-specific terms. Medical professionals employ vocation-specific

---

19. Ancient Christian experience has been divided into the "Apostolic Era," the "Sub-Apostolic Era," and the "Post-Apostolic Era" to help people get a handle on the church's developments and movements soon after inception. Churchmen stake out claims to the Christian past in order to gain rhetorical advantage by it in the present and to cast a vision for the future that they can more handily influence or control.

20. Given that many churchmen were disposed to see Messianic Jewish, Yeshua-believing adherents as "Christians" and "converts" who insignificantly happened to have been born Jewish, the appellative language that actually belonged to what one might call the original Messianic, *non*-Christian "Christians" fell into disuse (e.g., Nazarene, Ebionite, and the like), as did an overall awareness of their sensibilities.

language, as do legal professionals, scientists, educators, architects, accountants, and construction workers. Historians develop unique language, too. Everyone does it. Students of church history, ministry, and mission use similarly developed language. Christianized terms like B.C. and A.D., for example, were employed by a powerful church intent on defining time in accordance with its interests and priorities.

Centuries after Yeshua's death, burial, and resurrection, and through a rather strange twist of fate, Christianity became the principal religion of the Roman Empire. In conjunction, Latin church leaders sought to carve out space and time, arranging a sacred calendar akin to Judaism's. Summarized in Leviticus 23, for example, is Israel's calendar—which came replete with sacred days commemorating God's acts on their behalf in days past. Claiming its own triumphal emergence as the fulfillment of Israel's hope and the replacement of Israel's destiny, the reigning church developed a similar calendar and marked the decisive point in human history around Yeshua's emergence. Appreciative of his coming, I see no need to take issue with that in principle, but describing A.D. history with terms like ancient, medieval, and modern "Christian" periods, as is the case today, ignores the reality of the prior, present, and future Jewish history that is so central to a true understanding of Yeshua's coming.

These terms hinder the investigation of the Yeshua movement's Jewish origin and influence in the ancient Mediterranean world. Professor Stark gives four reasons why this Jewish presence is significant: (1) many of the converts in the New Testament were Hellenized Jews; (2) those converts were familiar with the Greek version of the Old Testament, called the Septuagint; (3) the earliest Christian missionaries frequented synagogues in the diaspora (i.e., in lands beyond Judea) to secure Jewish and Jewish-friendly converts—something they did well into the second century; and (4) archeological evidence shows that early Christian churches housing those converts outside "Palestine," to use his language, were concentrated in the Jewish sections of cities.[21]

Professor Stark is again helpful, despite his employment of anachronistic language. He correctly notes "the extent of Jewish conversion to Christianity during the first two centuries was [much] '*higher than is usually assumed.*'"[22] This sociologist of religion goes on to note that in "the middle of the second century the church was still *dominated by people with Jewish roots* and *strong current ties to the Jewish world.*"[23] Mindful of this, I agree with Dr. Mark Kinzer that we must be about "reaffirming our relationship to th[os]e Jewish people as a whole."[24] This, of course, is indeed desirable and long overdue, as is an overhaul of the perspective that the so-called "Christian sunrise" providentially cast a long shadow over Judaism and displaced Jewish influence and importance by the rays of its glorious grace. Though only passing reflections in his book, Dr. Stark's observation will be considered more fully in mine

21. Rodney Stark, *The Rise of Christianity: A Sociologist Reconsiders History*, p. 63.

22. Italics mine; in Robert S. MacLennan and A. Thomas Kraabel in "The God-Fearers—A Literary and Theological Invention." *Biblical Archeological Review* 12 (September-October, 1986), pp. 47–53. Culled from Rodney Stark, *The Rise of Christianity: A Sociologist Reconsiders History*, p. 67.

23. Italics mine; ibid., p. 65.

24. Mark Kinzer, "Toward a Theology of Messianic Judaism" in *Kesher: A Journal of Messianic Judaism* (Albuquerque: Union of Messianic Jewish Congregations, 2000), p. 106.

in order to, as Dr. Kinzer put it, *affirm the relationship*—even if few want to have it any longer.

Eager to construe the disparaged "Judaizing Church" (so called) as hopelessly and theologically out of step with the "new [post-Jewish] Christian era" by virtue of its assorted Judaistic proclivities, leaders in *both* synagogues and churches have been all too happy to marginalize, minimize, and anathematize ancient Messianic Jewish people and experience. Because I believe that this jaded view is both simplistic and problematic, this book presents a variety of resources that offer a decidedly Jewish-friendly account of early Christian history—what really is an extension of early Jewish history, and not a non-Messianic, "Christian" history at all.

We will begin by considering the Jerusalem-based Messianic Jewish movement, then proceed around the Mediterranean from there.

CHAPTER 2

JERUSALEM-BASED MESSIANIC JUDAISM

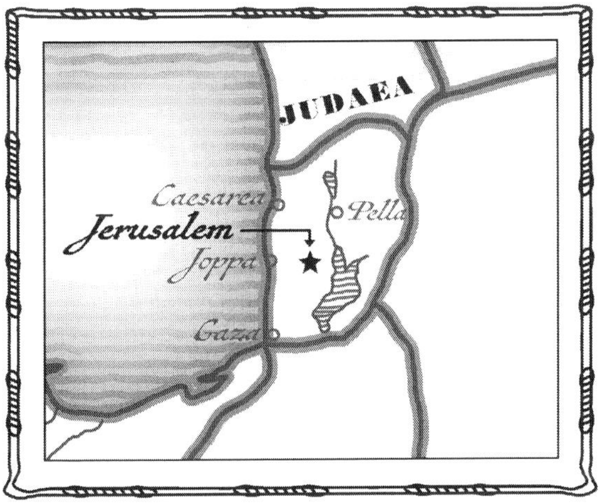

A Movement that Began in Jerusalem

Messianic Judaism—or early "Christianity," so called—came into its own in a first-century Jewish world wracked by political intrigue, social unrest, and misguided religious fervors. Messianic Judaism was one of various Israel-based movements that surfaced in response to external and internal pressures in Jewish social life. Some, like the Essenes (whom we have just come to know in the last century), withdrew and gave themselves over to eschatological speculation as they waited for God's eventual and direct intervention in human history. Less inclined to "wait it out" and see what God would do in time, others, like the "Zealots," wanted to take matters into their own hands. They traversed the city and the countryside alike, vociferously urging the weary populace to throw off the imperial Roman yoke of excessive taxation and political mismanagement that was facilitated in so many ways by ubiquitous religious apostasy. Yeshua and his *talmidim* (disciples) entered this boiling caldron with a more moderated message of peace and reconciliation. Though disconcerted by the current age, the Messianic movement placed more of a premium on a soon-coming, new era and advocated for flexibility in dealing with both Jews and the reigning non-Jewish power structures.

Like all Jews, Yeshua and his followers were deeply frustrated by Jewish aristocratic aloofness, religious treachery, and Roman insensitivity. They believed, however, that the social problems of the day would be fully and finally solved at the dawn of the Messianic era, and, for them, the morning had definitely broken.

Yeshua's half-brother Ya'akov, commonly known today by the name "James," was the Jerusalem-based Messianic movement's[1] first and principal leader. Mentioned early in New Testament literature in conjunction with the caustic,

1. I like referring to the church as a faith "*movement,*" as opposed to a *religious institution.* Writing in *Sociology of Early Palestinian Christianity*, Dr. Gerd Theissen posits that Yeshua called into being a "movement of wandering [miracle-working] charismatics" and that they were "not [simply] a marginal phenomenon." For Messianic Jews, signs and wonders served as evidence of the dawning of the new era; thus, the ability to perform healing and miracles was understandably the authenticating criterion for their leaders (see Mk. 16:17–18). Placed on the defensive by some who did not feel he had the "spiritual goods," in 1 Cor. 12:1, the traveling evangelist Rabbi Shaul (Paul) said "I'll go on to speak of visions and revelations," evidencing his spirituality. In v.11b he then retorts that he is "not the least inferior to [allegedly] superior apostles," and then offers evidence that he is God's representative: "the signs of a true apostle were performed among you... with signs and wonders and mighty works." (12:12) The importance of the miracle-working dimension of ministry for the earliest believers is well established in the *B'rit Hadasha* in a variety of ways. Evidence of miracle-working is found even beyond the pages of the New Testament.

disparaging taunts of the general disbelieving population (Mt. 13:55; Mk. 6:3), it seems that, at first, Ya'akov was not kindly disposed toward his half brother Yeshua (Jn. 7:5). However, things changed for him following what the New Testament reports as his half brother's death, burial, and resurrection. In the wake of Yeshua's execution, Ya'akov remained with his mother Miriam and the rest of his half brother's inner circle (Acts 1:14). Ya'akov had a special post-resurrection experience, where Yeshua personally manifested himself to him (1 Cor. 15:7). The late professor F. F. Bruce argued that this appearance must have had a profound and enduring "revolutionary effect" on Ya'akov.

A few years later, around 37 or 38 C.E., when Rabbi Shaul (called the Apostle Paul) visited Jerusalem, Ya'akov was resident there and was seated as the community's principal congregational leader. Upon his release from brief imprisonment in 44 C.E., Cephas (called Peter) made haste to get information to Ya'akov—which reveals Ya'akov's authority (Acts 12:17). By the time of the Jerusalem assembly around 52 C.E., Ya'akov was well established as the overseer of the Messianic movement (Acts 15:13–21). The meeting was convened to consider problems associated with Gentile inclusion in the Messianic movement. Luke says tensions were amicably resolved, affirmation and fellowship were formally extended to Shaul (i.e., Paul) by the Jerusalem leaders, with Ya'akov again referenced as one (Gal. 2:9). Lastly, in 58 C.E., when Shaul returned to Jerusalem following his third evangelistic journey in the *galut* (i.e., diaspora), he reported to Ya'akov (the primary congregational leader) who then made some suggestions to Shaul (Acts 21:17ff). It is clear that Ya'akov/James was the Jerusalem movement's principal leader.

In his *Ecclesiastical History*, Eusebius concurs and states "James the Just" (our Ya'akov) "… was the first to receive the episcopate of the church at Jerusalem" (*Ecc. Hist.* 2.1). The late Professor F. F. Bruce wrote that Eusebius used an early Messianic Jewish source called the *Acts of the Apostles*, a counterpart to Luke's volume, which presently (and mistakenly![2]) bears that name. Eusebius also quotes Clement who stated that both Peter and John preferred James, called "the Just," as the spiritual leader, even though all were given special gifts of knowledge (*Ecc. Hist.* 2.1). In recounting Ya'akov's martyrdom, Eusebius said the "Apostles committed the Episcopal seat to James" (*Ecc. Hist.* 2.23), indicating that the name "the Just" came to him by virtue of his personal Jewish faith and piety. Is it not interesting that the leader of the Messianic movement was known to be a pious Jew?

The case of Ya'akov's sway in Jerusalem is buttressed by the ecclesiastical historian Eusebius' citation from Hegeisippus, who flourished nearer to the days of the Apostles, and who stated that Ya'akov received the "government of the church," that he was comparable to a Nazarite in his strict religious observance, and perhaps by virtue of his being perceived as a *tzadik* (a righteous man) by his contemporaries, had access to the sanctuary proper. Professor Bruce notes, "James' assiduity in [Jewish] prayer within the holy precincts was public knowledge." Writing his *Antiquities* 20, the ancient Jewish historian Josephus tells of Ya'akov's execution, noting that it

2. I say "mistakenly" because it does not talk about the acts of the Apostles. Its emphasis is on Peter originally, after which the real reason becomes more apparent: The book is about the acts of the Apostle Paul—not about all the apostles.

was felt to be terribly unjust by many observant Jews, not just by Messianic believers. He clearly identifies this James (our Ya'akov) saying Annus the Sadducean high priest "convened the judges of the Sanhedrin and brought before them a man named James, the brother of Yeshua so called the Christ" (*Ant* 20.200).[3] After telling of Ya'akov's death in response to accusations and mob actions, Eusebius says Jerusalem's sack by Vespasian was understood by some, both Messianic Jews and non-believers alike, to have come in response to the unjust execution of the just one named Ya'akov (*Ecc. Hist.* 2 .23).

As for the manner of Ya'akov's premature death, Dr. Gerd Luedemann, Professor of New Testament and Director of the Institute of Early Christian Studies at the University of Gottingen, Germany, offers the following from a comparison of extant ancient source texts. Ya'akov is reported to have given a stirring speech in the Temple complex in defense of his half-brother's claim to be the gateway to heaven (cf. Jn. 14:6). A tumult broke out and Ya'akov kept speaking, prompting members of the ruling religious elite to take punitive action on the spot. Ya'akov was thrown from the Temple and was beaten and stoned, all the while making intercession for his tormentors, until death came from the severe blow of a fuller's club, an ancient instrument used to beat fabrics.

Following Ya'akov's execution and Jerusalem's capture, Eusebius states that the brethren handpicked Simon, son of Cleophas, another Jewish believer, to lead the Jerusalem congregation (Ecc *Hist.* 3. 11), a fact corroborated by him later when he gave a full telling of all the Messianic Jewish leaders in Jerusalem (*Ecc. Hist.* 4.5; cf. 7.19).

---

3. Remember that because Josephus is not a believer in Yeshua, one cannot expect him to speak of Him with the reverence of a believer.

The Messianic Movement's Headquarters in Jerusalem

During Israel's Independence War in 1948, Mount Zion and its environs became the staging area for a considerable amount of fighting between Israeli and Jordanian forces. In the course of the escalating hostilities, a mortar inadvertently fell on the site of David's tomb, exposing an area previously hidden from view. An Israeli archeologist, Dr. Jacob Pinkerfield, eventually excavated the site in 1951 and likely discovered the oldest Messianic synagogue in Jerusalem in the process. Writing in *Biblical Archeological Review* (May/June 1990), Dr. Bargil Pixner told the story of the archeological find in his article entitled "Church of the Apostles Found in Mount Zion."

Dr. Pixner reported that underneath the existing flooring, Dr. Pinkerfield found a twelfth-century Byzantine period. Just four inches beneath the Byzantine mosaic he uncovered the remains of a synagogue's flooring, dating back to the first century C.E. On this particular stratum, he found inscriptions on plaster, which were eventually made public by Franciscan scholars Testa and Bagatti at the Stadium Biblicum Franciscanum. One of the first-century inscriptions translates "O Jesus, that I may live," "conquer, Savior, mercy."

Alas, a Messianic synagogue in Jerusalem!

As was and is common for synagogues, the structure's niche, where the Torah was kept, faced the Temple Mount generally—but not exactly. While it faced the Temple Mount direction, it was oriented precisely toward what became the site of the Church of the Sepulcher, the area then believed to be the place of Yeshua's death, burial, and resurrection. The implications of the subtle shift are noteworthy and thought-provoking.

Known today by Jews as the site of King David's tomb, the site is also referred to by the Catholic Christians as the Church of the Apostles. Their case is built in part on the testimony of Epiphanius, a fourth-century bishop, who said, "In Hadrian's day there stood a small Church of God. It marked the site of the Upper Room to which the disciples returned from the Mount of Olives…." (*Treatise on Weights and Measurements* 14).[4] Epiphanius states the Messianic Jews headquartered there "did not give themselves the name of Christ (i.e., being called 'Christians,' the common appellation today) but preferred being called 'Nazarenes'" (1–2). "By birth they are Jews" who, after "having seen the divine signs performed by the hands of the Apostles believed in Jesus" (5–6, cf. 4,9). Though

4. This "small room" was arguably a Messianic synagogue. This belief is corroborated by Euthychius, the tenth-century patriarch of Alexandria, who writes that Jewish believers "returned to Jerusalem in the fourth year of the Emperor Vespasian, and built there their church." In his *Demonstrato Evangelica*, Eusebius writes that the "Gospel is poured forth from Jerusalem and Mount Zion adjacent to it," likely a reference to the aforementioned synagogue. Eucherius, a converted Roman senator who became archbishop of Lyons, comments that "the plain upper part [of Mount Zion] is occupied by monks' cells which surround the church. Its foundations, it is said, have been laid by the Apostles…." In 384, Cyril, bishop of Jerusalem, delivered a famous speech in the then newly constructed Church of the Sepulcher, and said that "it would have been more appropriate to speak about the Holy Spirit in the very place where the Holy Spirit descended … in the upper church of the Apostles," not at the Church of the Sepulcher. Why then did not Cyril speak in the original Messianic synagogue, since he apparently knew of it? Epiphanius, a fourth-century bishop of Jewish extraction, gives the answer: the Messianic synagogue had been "cut off" (as heretical) by the reigning Roman church. Dr. Robert Milburn, professor of church history at Oxford University, says that the Roman church was seen as a symbol of the Roman Christian supplanting of the Temple and the ancient [Jewish] law. Patristic sources relate that, in response to the anti-Judaic rhetoric, a Messianic Jewish bishop of Gaza known as Saint Porphyrius sought to reconcile the two congregations—the Messianic Jews and the non-Jewish Christians. In keeping with this spirit, in 387 John II, the bishop of Jerusalem from 387–419, even went so far as to bless the altar of the Messianic Jews and refer to it as the kapporet! Sadly, the attempt at reconciliation ultimately failed!

they "believed" in Yeshua, the Messianic Jews remained problematic, according to Epiphanius personally and all non-Jewish believers generally, because they "remained wholly Jewish and nothing else" (7,1). "For they," observes Epiphanius in the fourth century, "use not only the New Testament but also the Old *like the Jews. …*" (italics mine; 7,2). For Epiphanius and others, this is shocking! He goes on to convey that this "heresy of the Nazarenes exists in Beroea in the neighborhood of Coele Syria and the Decapolis in the region of Pella… [for] from there it took its beginning after the Exodus from Jerusalem when all the disciples went to live in Pella … since it [Jerusalem] was about to undergo a siege" (7–8).

Given their recalcitrance and Jewish affinities, Epiphanius says that they are "under a curse" from God, for their attempts to "keep the Shabbat and circumcision" (8,1). We will hear more from him later. That being "like the Jews" was sadly construed as problematic was also evidenced by St. Jerome's saying that Jews and their prayers were *grunnitus suis et clamos asinorium* (i.e., "the grunting of pigs and the crying of donkeys").

Not only were "grunting" Messianic Jews alleged by Epiphanius to be "cut off" by and from God, but the pigs were also deemed unkosher by other Jews. In 9,2 he says that Messianic Jews are "very much hated by the Jews. For not only did the Jewish children cherish hate against them, according to him, but the people also stood up in the morning, at noon, and in the evening, three times a day, to pronounce curses and maledictions over them. "Jewish hatred of them," according to Epiphanius, is said in 9,3 to be because "they proclaim as Jews that Jesus is the Christ [a claim], which runs counter to those who still are Jews who do not accept

Jesus." For his part, St. Augustine parrots Epiphanius' anti-Messianic views and offers a fitting final corroboration in his treatise *de Baptismo contra Donatist*ais: "…they persist to the present day who call themselves Nazarene Christians and circumcise the carnal foreskin in a Jewish way. [These are] born heretics…" (VII 1,1).[5]

In sum, it is to be observed that a vibrant Messianic Jewish movement flourished in Judea before the first Roman war and that it was established there afresh immediately after the debacle. The ancients also note that the movement flourished in Judea till the second Jewish-Roman war. Though there had been a vibrant Jewish expression of Messianic faith, things began to change. Over time, and owing to the Gospel's expansion to non-Jews in the broader culture, the Empire was "Christianized" by a Roman church that saw itself alone as representative of the New Chosen People of God! In the wake of this, Messianic Jews were denigrated and displaced, seen only as the reigning church's ancient vanquished rival, leftover fruits from a condemned system. Jewishness was despised—the message of Israel's Messiah was framed exclusively in non-Jewish terms and given a non-Jewish expression. This situation prevailed well into the present modern era and is now slowly being addressed by bold women and men bent on investigating legitimate biblical forms of Jewish faith and worship and integrating them with appropriate Christian symbols, literature, and language.

---

5. Writing in *Nazarene Jewish Christianity: From the End of the New Testament Period Until Its Disappearance in the Fourth Century,* Dr. Ray Pritz says that the "Augustine [bishop] of Hippo marks a decisive point in the history of the church's view of the Nazarenes. While Epiphanius was the first to brand them as heretical, it was the authority of Augustine's acceptance of this judgment which seems to have fixed their fate and led to their final rejection by the church" at large.

Chapter 3

The Demise of Jerusalem-Based Messianic Judaism

Introduction

As noted previously, Messianic Judaism came into its own in a very precarious world, one wracked by political intrigue and social unrest. The vibrant Messianic Jewish faith movement that was both birthed and established in Jerusalem during those very troubling times was propagated *through* and *to* Torah-observant Jewish people, and—as we shall see—was advanced to Jewish-friendly Gentiles, from there.

Pressing circumstances were imposed upon Judean social life in the late 60s C.E. not long after the movement's inception.

Some years later, and within a hundred years of its birth, another and even more devastating war caused total upheaval in the lives of many Messianic Jews. In the aftermath of the dread Bar Kochba Revolt of the second century C.E. (see below), the Jewish capital was totally gobbled up by "dogs of war," given to trampling Jews under foot. Jews were then forbidden access to Jerusalem, which meant the city was not able to serve as the spiritual center for the Jewish people, nor as a center for the fledgling Messianic Jewish movement—which was a prophetic voice to and for the Jewish people.

Professors Anson Rainey, of Tel Aviv University, and R. Steven Notley, of Nyack College, explain succinctly:

> In the aftermath of the Bar Kochba Revolt, the Jewish population in the land of Israel was [utterly] decimated. Many Jews who previously resided in the land emigrated to the diaspora... [The land of Israel experienced] a greater influx of non-Jewish people.[1]

Gentiles came.

Jews left.

Where did the Jews go?

The Judean deserts and wilderness to the east and south were not particularly hospitable. While traversing the Sinai and making their way to Alexandria, Egypt (where there already was a significant Jewish population) might have been a choice, *there's a cogent argument that the better part of the*

1. Anson F. Rainey and R. Steven Notley, *The Sacred Bridge* (Jerusalem: Carta 2006), p. 398.

Jewish population shifted north—to the Galilee and beyond, *with Syria and its environs playing host to untold multitudes.*[2]

Thus, they went to the area at Israel's northernmost border, the Levant—among other places.

After noting Antioch's rise as a center for Jews on the move, in his *Backgrounds of Early Christianity*, Professor Everett Ferguson of Abilene Christian University went on to report how "fairly large numbers of Jews were [once] moved by Hellenistic monarchs to Asia Minor,"[3] our present Turkey. In his "Christianity in Edessa and the Syriac-Speaking World… The Struggle for Allegiance on the Aramean Frontier," Catholic University of America's Professor Sidney Griffith notes that wars…were an "ever-present factor" in ancient Syria, with the world "constantly shifting" and with the "often forced transfer of whole populations from one jurisdiction to the other depending on the fortunes of war."[4] Mindful of both scholars' observations, we will consider what circumstances forced Jews to leave Judea proper and make their way to and through the Levant.

How Messianic Jews thought, and how they lived in the Levant, will be subjected to some analysis. In what follows immediately, however, we will briefly turn our attention to the

---

2. Professor Robinson speaks of potential "mobile groups" and asserts that, based on an observation that the distance from Jerusalem is the same for both Alexandria and Antioch, they would have preferred Antioch since the land was much closer to what agricultural Jews were used to. [Thomas A. Robinson, *Ignatius of Antioch and the Parting of the Ways: Early Jewish-Christian Relations* (Peabody: Hendrickson, 2009), p. 35.]

3. Everett Ferguson, *Backgrounds of Early Christianity* (Grand Rapids: Eerdmans Publishing Company, 1993), p. 380.

4. Sidney Griffith, "Christianity in Edessa and the Syriac-Speaking World: Mani, Bar Daysan and Ephraem; The Struggle for Allegiance on the Aramean Frontier" (www.sage.edu/faculty/salomd/ld/ Edessa.htm), p. 4.

tensions that caused Judean Messianic Jews to flee the capital, taking begrudging leave of their place of origin—for many, many centuries to follow.

The First Roman Revolt

In the mid-first century C.E., tensions flared in Judea in response to news that the emperor Caligula intended to set up a statue of his own in the Jerusalem Temple. Disconcerted Jews and anti-Semitic Greeks came to blows in Caesarea as a result; riots then spread inland and to Jerusalem proper. News reached King Agrippa II who attempted to put a lid on the cascading unrest, but his hollow appeals for calm proved unfruitful.[5] Seeing an opportunity to seize the moment by exploiting the unrest for his own purposes, the nefarious and provocative procurator Gessius Florus (64–66 C.E.) was all too happy to fan the flames of discontent. Perturbed by Florus' incessant abuses, chagrined Judeans appealed to the Roman governor in Antioch, a legate named Cestius Gallus. Their appeals fell on deaf ears, however, and they were unable to get redress for their grievances. Unmitigated Jewish discontent ran its course, with the result that pent-up furies were spent on the rapid mobilization of ad hoc Jewish militia. Upon learning of this, and by way of response, Gallus disembarked from his headquarters in Antioch with the Legion XII Fulminata (meaning the "Thundering One") along with two thousand regulars from other Syrian-based legions—

5. His father, Agrippa I, was the Herodian monarch who persecuted Jewish believers in Judea and who killed Ya'akov/James (Acts 12:1–2), and whose son gave Gallus his willing hand. Luke records Agrippa I's death by stomach "worms" in Acts 12:19–23, which correlates with Josephus' account of his being "gripped in his stomach by an ache" in *Ant.* 19:346. This martyr-maker was survived by a few daughters and a young son, Agrippa II, under whose subsequent administration the entire Jewish kingdom was handed over to the ultimate supervision of the governor of Syria—Gallus, previously noted.

e.g., the Legion III Galicia, the VI Ferrata and the X Fretensis—to put a lid on the revolt. Unlike his father Agrippa I (who had more pious Jewish inclinations), Agrippa II seemed little more than a Roman proxy at the core. The Syrian-tied Agrippa II[6] supplied foot soldiers and cavalry to assist Gallus in getting the better of his own Jewish people.[7]

Gallus' XII "Fulminata" proved to be more thunder than striking lightning, at the outset. The Legion not only lost its striking power, it even lost its symbol: the "eagle." Bested by circumstances and shamed by its losses, the floundering XIIth was forced to retreat from Jerusalem. The initial triumph over the Romans encouraged Jewish masses, many of which construed the turn of events in their favor as a signal that Providence was shining upon them and giving them miraculous favor—finally. Pent-up religious hopes and aspirations were inflamed. Intoxicated by the encouragement, they geared up for an all-out eschatological contest with the Romans, assured of their ultimate victory in the otherwise suicidal war. Jews controlled Judea—for the moment, anyway. Jewish military forces set up their own administration in a capital that was just miraculously wrested from Roman control; they minted their own coins, and they divided the country into military districts. They readied themselves for Rome's response, believing prophecy was being fulfilled in their day. The response was forthcoming.[8]

---

6. *Ant.* 19:363–365; *War* 2:220; culled from Anson F. Rainey and R. Steven Notley, *The Sacred Bridge*, p. 384, my principal source for the reconstruction of events culminating in the destruction of Judea in the first and second wars.

7. According to Tacitus, he had previously sent troops to assist the Romans in their campaign against the Parthians. (See *Ann.* 13.)

8. Yohannan Aharoni and Michael Avi-Yonah, *The MacMillan Bible Atlas, Revised* (New York: Macmillan Publishing Company, 1977), p. 157.

Vespasian was apprised of the situation at his eastern front. To Gallus' initial-response forces, Vespasian added the Legion XV Apollinaris, called up by his son Titus, who was dispatched to Alexandria, Egypt, for the very purpose of mobilizing more forces for the Judean campaign. Some time after the initial outbreak and response, Vespasian traveled overland and proceeded to Syria where he marshaled these and other forces to ensure success in quelling the Judean revolt which, till then, wasn't going as Rome had hoped.

Jewish responses to Vespasian's arrival in Syria in 67 C.E. were mixed. Expecting that some Jews in Antioch would naturally be loyal to their associates in Jerusalem, and thus supportive of their bid to throw off the Roman yoke, non-Jews were increasingly on edge. Old anti-Jewish prejudices prompted new anti-Jewish suspicions among some, resulting in, among other things, a charge that Jewish insurgents started a major fire that broke out in Antioch. Given to due process, Rome investigated and the matter cleared the Jews. Mucianus, governor of Syria from 67–69 C.E., exonerated the Jews in Antioch over and against the objections of prejudiced locals determined to disparage the Jewish population.

Just to the south of Syria, in Israel proper, encouragement from initial efforts to stave off the Roman forces in Jerusalem proved to be short-lived. Not inclined to let the insult go unanswered and simply settle with their losses, Roman forces were reconstituted and galvanized under Vespasian. Invigorated by new energies, they re-launched their assault and began getting the better of the Jewish revolutionaries.

Vibrations from the Roman armies' approaching drumbeats created no small stir among the Jewish people—*prompting mass evacuations,* even before the great eschatological war was officially contested and decided in Jerusalem. Beginning in the north in the Galilee and then moving south to Judea, as the Romans advanced, many Jews rushed to get out of their way. Displaced persons were effectually relegated to the status of refugees and were forced to flee north to Syria to find and rebuild their lives.

Writing "The Jewish-Christians' Move from Jerusalem as a Pragmatic Choice" in *Studies in Rabbinic Judaism and Early Christianity*, Dr. Jonathan Bourgel, a postdoctoral candidate at Tel Aviv University at the time of the writing, postulates that, with many, many other Jewish peoples and groups, Jewish believers in Yeshua surrendered to the Romans who then resettled them in Pella. In support of this compelling hypothesis, Bourgel alights upon Josephus' mention that Vespasian gave "his right hand for their preservation," a reference to those who came over to him during the war (*Wars*, 4.130 and 444). This conciliatory move was similarly followed by Titus (*Wars*, 4.115) and then Placidus (*Wars*, 4. 438).[9] "It appears," says Dr. Bourgel, "that the phenomenon of desertions from Jerusalem increased as Vespasian completed the surrounding of the city."[10] In support, Josephus is further cited in *Wars* 4.377 where "on numerous occasions large numbers of people fled from the city to seek refuge with the Romans."[11] Josephus encouraged Jews to do just that, as he himself did, to the chagrin of many afterwards—and for centuries to follow.

9. Dan Jaffee (ed.), *Studies in Rabbinic Judaism and Early Christianity: Text and Context* (Leiden/Boston: Brill, 2010), p. 119. Dr. Bourgel is the principal source for my reconstruction of the argument, along with Professors Rainey and Notley. (See below.)

10. Ibid., p. 123.

11. Ibid. and p. 129; see also *Wars* 4.397, 410.

Was the abandonment a result of betrayal? *Not at all!* "Internal upheavals led to the departure of many" disconcerted Jews,[12] as frenzied and murderous Zealots usurped power in Jerusalem and took control of the struggle. Josephus is very clear on this matter: "*Many there were of the Jews that deserted every day, and fled away from the Zealots*" (Italics mine; *Wars*, 4.377). They would have particularly threatened Jewish believers in Yeshua, when those "assassins" took over the city in the late spring of 68 C.E. just before Vespasian completed surrounding it in June of the same year.

For their part, Professors Rainey and Notley agree and state that it could very well be at this time when the Messianic Jews, who stayed on in Jerusalem for a season (*with many other Jews*), eventually left Jerusalem for Pella, Jordan, as noted by Eusebius in his *Eccl. Hist.* 3.5.2–3:

> The people of the church in Jerusalem were commanded by an oracle given by revelation before the war, to those in the city who were worthy of it, to depart and dwell in one of the cities of Perea, which they called Pella.

To this account, Epiphanius later added:

> When the city was about to be taken by the Romans…they sojourned to Pella… in Transjordan. But afterward they returned (*Treatise on Weights and Measurements* 15).

12. Ibid., p. 124.

By conflating all three historians' accounts we learn that Messianic Jews eventually left Jerusalem because of the war—*not at the very outset*—when the Zealots came to power and when Jerusalem's demise became apparent in the second wave of the Roman assault. *After the war, "they returned" to Jerusalem*, to their ancestral homeland and to the place of their affections. Speaking of "affections," Dr. Bourgel concludes that "the migration to Pella did *not* lead to the religious separation between Jewish-Christians and their Jewish brethren as several scholars have proposed… [and that] it *cannot* be considered as an abandoning of their Jewish identity or of their religious beliefs."[13]

Professor Eyal Regev, of the Department of Land of Israel Studies and Archeology of the Bar-Ilan University, concurs. He observed how Christians have "tended to presume (without demonstration) [that the New Testament has] a completely negative approach toward the Temple, seeing Yeshua as having completely "*substituted*" it, as per Dr. D. Juel, as having "*condemned*" its "corruption," according to Dr. W. H. Kelber, and as bringing "to an end its commercial and cultic activities" according to Dr. F. J. Moloney.[14] Leaning lastly on Professor E. P. Sanders, he reminds "nothing Jesus said or did which bore on the Law led his disciples after his death to disregard it," i.e., Temple participation.[15] *Fidelity to the ancestral religion is evident everywhere,* as we shall see.

13. Italics mine; Ibid., p. 134.

14. Italics mine; "The Temple in Mark: A Case Study About the Early Christian Attitude Toward the Temple," pp. 139–140.

15. Ibid., p. 155; from Sanders, *Jesus and Judaism,* p. 268. Worth noting is that Jewish scholars seem to prefer promoting the misunderstanding. See Professor Cook, above, from Hebrew Union College.

Josephus records that the Temple was destroyed on the 10th of Av, 70 C.E. in *War* 6:250—*not* on the 9th. That aside, and in the wake of the Temple's demise in the aftermath of the war, "Titus left the Legion X Fretensis in Jerusalem, while stationing the Legion XII Fulminata, besides the Euphrates near the confines of Armenia and Cappadocia" and retained the Legions V Macedonia and XV Apollinaris with himself (*War* 7.17–19).[16] This was the deathblow, to be sure.

Though commemorated for all time in the "Arch of Triumph in Rome," in the immediate aftermath of the war and before making it to Rome with their spoils, Vespasian's son Titus (who took charge of the campaign) went through Syria to Antioch where he celebrated the victory by displaying Jewish captives and prizes of war. In *Wars* 7.96, Josephus says he "exhibited costly spectacles in all the cities of Syria." This, no doubt, would have put the many Jewish residents there in an awkward position, despite their not having participated in the revolt themselves.

Josephus reported on the condition in Syria after the war. "The whole of Syria," says he, "was a scene of frightful disorder, every city was divided into two camps… each city had its Judaizers who aroused suspicion" (*Wars* 2.462–3). Language-defining Jews, Jewish believers in Yeshua, Gentile believers, Orthodox Judaism, and Christianity had *not* yet developed. That being so, an expression like "*Judaizers* who aroused suspicion" draws some suspicion, warrants some special attention, and will be considered later—when Dr. Magnus Zetterholm of Lund University, Sweden, theorizes that they were actually enthusiastic Gentiles with affinities for

16. Anson F. Rainey and R. Steven Notley, *The Sacred Bridge,* p. 394.

things Jewish. (He sees "Gentile Jesus-believers cloaked as Jews,"[17] as opposed to their being Jewish-believing, Messianic Jews or religious Jewish enthusiasts within mainstream Jewish culture.[18]) More on this later.

The Second Roman Revolt

Returning to the historical record, and speaking of the First Revolt's aftermath in Judea, Epiphanius noted that "afterward" (i.e., after the first revolt), Jewish believers "returned" to Judea. Their homeward bound movement was further noted by Eusebius, who referred to Messianic Jewish presence and leadership in Jerusalem in his *Ecc. Hist.* 4, 5:2. There, he is explicit in noting their presence until the invasion of Adrian/ Hadrian to quell the Bar Kochba Revolt, from 132–135 C.E.—*the debacle that forced their displacement,* with all others:

> [D]own to the invasion of the Jews under Adrian, there were fifteen successions of bishops in the church, all of which they say were Hebrews...at the time the whole church under them consisted of faithful Hebrews, who continued from the time of the apostles until the siege that then took place.

Eusebius notes the presence of Messianic Jews in Jerusalem until the early second century and underscores that the mother-of-all-fellowship's leadership was in Jewish hands, until the Bar Kochba war put an end to Jewish presence in the area.

17. Magnus Zetterholm, *The Formation of Christianity in Antioch: A Social-Scientific Approach to the Separation between Judaism and Christianity,* p. 205.
18. Consider Rev. 3:9, where noted are "those who say they are Jews but are not."

As noted previously, Euthychius, the tenth-century patriarch of Alexandria, claimed that Jewish believers had "returned to Jerusalem in the fourth year of the emperor Vespasian, and built there their church,"[19] on Mount Zion. Writing in *Demonstratio Evangelica*, Eusebius referenced that the Gospel is "poured forth from Jerusalem and Mount Zion adjacent to it,"[20] i.e., from the headquarters of the Messianic Jews. Eucherius, a Roman senator who converted to Christianity and became the archbishop of Lyons, referenced Jerome when speaking of a place of worship on Mount Zion, then "occupied by monks," but which initially was "said to have been laid by the [Messianic Jewish] Apostles" themselves.[21] In 384 C.E., Cyril, bishop of Jerusalem, spoke of newer facilities built atop the ruins of the earlier headquarters of the Messianic Jews in Jerusalem.

What happened? What made Messianic Judaism but a memory—a "ruin"?

The Jerusalem branch of the Messianic movement ended in Jerusalem when Jerusalem ended for the Messianic Jews. Messianic believers did *not* speedily abandon Jews in the first revolt, nor did they casually depart in the second. After the

---

19. See Jeffrey L. Seif, *Evolution of a Revolution: Reflections on Ancient Christianity in Its Judaistic, Hellenistic and Romanistic Expressions* (Lanham: University Press of America, 1994), p. 35; culled from Bargil Pixner's "Church of the Apostles Found on Mount Zion," in *Biblical Archeological Review*, p. 26; from Migne, ed., *Patrologia* Vol. III (Parris, 1844), p. 985.

20. See Jeffrey L. Seif, *Evolution of a Revolution: Reflections on Ancient Christianity in its Judaistic, Hellenistic and Romanistic Expressions,* p. 35; Baldi, *Enchiridion Locorum Sanctorum* (Jerusalem: Franciscan Printing Press, 1982), reprint from the second edition, p. 728.

21. Ibid.

decimation of the Temple in 70 C.E. in the first war, Jerusalem was renamed Aelia Capitolina and a temple dedicated to Jupiter was placed on the mount. Messianic Jews left late and returned early, opting to live in proximity to the desecrated Temple Mount—as did other Jewish returnees.

Dio Cassius said, "Vespasian ordered that Jews who continued to observe their ancestral customs should pay an annual tribute of two denarii" to the pagan shrine, in this case (65.7.2). Messianic Jews would have paid this, though begrudgingly—with many other Jews. Once the fee for Temple maintenance, its continual collection would have been a further affront to Jewish sensibilities given that the "*denarii duo Judarorum*" was now affixed to finance the temple dedicated to *Jupiter Capitolinus*. Further, Dio Cassius says the Bar Kochba Revolt, the second war, was initiated because "the Jews deemed it intolerable that foreign races should be settled in their city and foreign religious rites planted there." (Dio Cass. 69.12.1–2) While this may indeed be true, professors Rainey and Notley believe it to be untenable—as does this writer. "Since Titus' conquest of Jerusalem in 70 C.E., the Legion X Fretensis had been garrisoned within the confines of Jerusalem. Thus a Roman presence in the holy city after sixty years can hardly have been the cause of a sudden insurrection,"[22] according to them.

The lingering tax issue for the desecrating shrine, and all that went with it, could have been particularly problematic. Others consider Emperor Hadrian's vacillation as the primary cause. Though initially intending to assist with the building

22. Ibid., p. 396.

of a new Jewish Temple in Jerusalem in 130 C.E., he was said to have changed his mind after visiting Jerusalem. Thus, he went ahead with its reconstitution as an offensive, decidedly non-Jewish city. Chagrined, some Jews started stockpiling weapons and plotting revenge, under the leadership of Simon Bar Kochba. Messianic Jews would have taken issue and stood with him, till he claimed himself the "Messiah." Then, of course, they would have been unable to position themselves under his banner. In any case, in the wake of his failed revolt, the province known as Iudaea was renamed *Syria Palaestina,* with perennial Jewish banishment as punishment for the insurrection—except for "visiting rights" on the ninth of Av.

While the reasons for the second revolt are both varied and debated, the consequences are not: *Jews were subsequently forbidden access to Jerusalem—and this meant Messianic Jews, too.* Eusebius sums up the Messianic believers' banishment, in *Hist. Eccl.* 4, 6:4:

> …when the city came to be bereft of the nation of the Jews, and its ancient inhabitants had completely perished, foreigners of the Church colonized it, too, it was composed of Gentiles, and after the Jewish bishops, the first who was appointed to minister there was Marcus.

Eusebius says Jews "completely perished" as an entity in Jerusalem, and that the church that eventually was reconstituted there was made up of non-Jews.[23] Given all the above, students of Messianic Jewish history must begrudgingly turn their attention from the Holy City of Jerusalem.

Though Jews seem to have perished as an entity in Jerusalem, they did not perish as an entity in Israel. Professor Eric M. Meyers teamed up with Professor James F. Strange and wrote *Archeology, the Rabbis & Early Christianity*,"[24] where they noted how older Catholic Church buildings were built atop synagogues—better "Messianic" synagogues.

In Capernaum, for example, just down the street from a very large and very old traditional synagogue sits an octagonal church facility built atop ruins said to have once been "St.

23. Weakened by strife over the years, the Hasmonean rule in Judea ended in 37 B.C.E., when the Roman senate confirmed Herod the Great as king of Judea. Herod subsequently built the Antonia Fortress adjacent to the Temple's northwestern corner, in addition to which he built a theater and hippodrome—projects at the beginning of their presence. Herod's most famous project, however, was the Temple complex itself—a marvel to behold, and the pride of Judea. The renovation project began in 20 B.C.E. and was completed during the procuratorship of Albinus (62–64 C.E.). Josephus said that the project employed 11,000 workers. It was indeed a marvel to behold—evidenced today by remains of the Herodian ashlar stones, ruins from the Royal Stoa, remains of Robinson's Arch, excavations from the street running along the western and southern walls, Warren's shaft, the Huldah Gates, and more. Architectural marvels did not assuage the Jews' disdain for the interloper Herod. Jews wanted neither Roman rulers nor their client kings, so the aforementioned war broke out in the wake of their provocation. The Roman V, X, XII, and XV legions were brought in to quell the rebellion, with the X legion staying on in the wake of the revolt's quelling. In fact, as noted, that legion was securely garrisoned in Jerusalem thereafter for hundreds of years. In 130 C.E., the Emperor Hadrian (117–138 C.E.) founded a Roman pagan city atop Jerusalem's ruins, which he named Aelia Capitolina. Aelia was named after the emperor himself (Publius Aelius Hadrianus); Capitolina refers back to the Capitoline gods (i.e., Jupiter, Juno, and Minerva). Jerusalem was divided into two sectors: to the south was the longstanding headquarters of the tenth legion camp, and the northern section was the urban-civilian area. The Jewish city ceased being Jewish, and the rest is history.

24. Eric Meyers and James F. Strange, *Archeology, the Rabbis & Early Christianity* (Nashville: Abingdon Press, 1981), p. 125.

Peter's house." Despite being unable to comprehend how a poor day laborer like Peter could afford a seaside residence, one just off the main street in ancient Capernaum, there is reason to grant that there is something of importance there.

Dr. Meyers and Dr. Strange assessed the site and, with the excavators, concluded, "Sometime near the end of the first century C.E." the facility underwent "conversion to a public building,"[25] and became a *domus-ecclesia* (i.e., "house church"). Beyond the plaster evidence undergirding their case, "pilgrims...incising graffiti of Christian character on the plastered walls" reveals its public nature, prompting the authors to conclude, "we have, provisionally speaking, the oldest Christian sanctuary unearthed anywhere" there.[26] Calling it a "Christian" site obscures the fact that it would have been a synagogue, and the people there Jews. Perhaps a consideration of another extremely famous archeological site in the Galilee just down the road will bring the point home more.

In Nazareth sits another famous Roman Catholic shrine, one that has been adored by enthusiasts of the Virgin Mary for many, many years. Many who adore the Jewish handmaiden ignore the fact that the famous Catholic "Basilica of the Annunciation" sits over an ancient Jewish synagogue.

Beneath part of the fifth-century C.E. Byzantine church is a *mikveh*—i.e., a Jewish ritual bath. Dr. Meyers and Dr. Strange make much of this in their accounting. Beyond that, a mosaic located in close proximity came with the inscription, "Offering of Conon, Deacon of Jerusalem." Excavators assume this to be the namesake of the famous martyr of Nazareth killed in the

25. Ibid., p. 129.
26. Ibid., p. 130.

Decian persecution (249–251 c.e.), who is reported as saying at his trial, "I am of the city of Nazareth in Galilee. I am of the family of Christ, to whom I offer a cult from the time of my ancestors." Giving credence to his Jewish heritage (e.g., speaking of the "time of my ancestors") must surely impress itself upon students of early Messianic Jewish beginnings.

Beyond this, "when the Mosaic was lifted, the excavators discovered that this mosaic fragment partially covered an ancient basin, probably a[nother] ritual bath (*mikveh*)."[27] More fascinating still, in the famous Catholic Basilica of the Annunciation, excavators found "abutments of double arches with carefully cut moldings… [that] most closely resemble those from synagogues of the Galilee and Golan Heights," which prompts the professors to conclude that either the community dismantled a synagogue and reused the stones or it was a synagogue at some point. One wonders if they smiled when they reported that "pilgrims scratched… prayers of a Christian character, even in the stones of a synagogue."[28] They conclude later, "it seems inescapable that the synagogue had become a church,"[29] or, with Father Bagatti, it was "Jewish-Christian from the beginning."[30]

In either case, the fact that historic churches associated with Peter and Mary are built over synagogue ruins gives credence to the fact that after the destruction of Jerusalem, Jewish believers in Yeshua continued on in the Galilee—and for quite some time, it seems.

27. Ibid., p. 132.
28. Ibid., p. 134.
29. Ibid., p. 135.
30. Ibid., p. 136.

In time, however, Messianic Jewish experience took hold more in the north, and in lands beyond. Much as Messianic Jewish believers continued in northern Israel, so too, Jews continued to greatly multiply elsewhere in the Roman Empire.

Dr. Rodney Stark points out that we should "keep in mind how greatly the Hellenized Jews of the diaspora outnumbered the Jews living in Palestine,"[31] in the first place, even before the great wars reduced large segments of their ranks. Dr. Paul Johnson suggests there were one million Jews in Judea and four million outside, whereas Dr. Wayne Meeks claims there were five to six million Jews living outside in the broader Greco-Roman world.[32] The point is clear: *Jews had a life outside of Israel.*

We will now take leave of Israel and follow the vanquished Jewish people to the north and to the west. There we will acquaint ourselves with their new resting places—and hear the restless voices they raised from them.

---

31. Rodney Stark, *The Rise of Christianity: A Sociologist Reconsiders History*, p. 57.
32. Ibid.

CHAPTER 4

JEWISH INFLUENCES IN THE LEVANTINE CULTURE AND CONGREGATIONS

Introduction

If the extant sources are to be believed, in the first century C.E., a fledgling Jewish renewal movement came into its own in and around Jerusalem. Its principal actors came from the country's northernmost region, one that borders Syria geographically and was connected to it politically—called the Galilee. In time and through circumstance, however, the Messianic movement's headquarters transitioned to Israel's capital city to the south. Prominent though Jerusalem was, not long after inception, and as a result of the ravages of two distinct revolts, the Messianic movement's principal and most active headquarters transitioned to a much larger, more distant city, one located 250 miles to the north of Jerusalem in Antioch.

Though the Messianic Jewish movement initially took root in Jerusalem, the ancient fledgling movement was uprooted from there a few decades later. Jerusalem was the movement's first camp, but Antioch became the Messianic movement's principal foreign base camp during the Jerusalem era, and then the principal headquarters for the movement after Jewish believers were uprooted from Jerusalem. That being the case, considering how the Messianic movement's story played out in Antioch and in the broader region[1] holds out significant promise—thus the purpose for this book.

It is said that Antioch had a population of 400,000–500,000 at the time, making it one of the four largest cities in the known world along with Rome, Italy; Alexandria, Egypt; and Carthage in North Africa. Much as Jerusalem was very important to Jewish people, Antioch was particularly important to the Greeks and then the Romans for reasons that were much more material than spiritual.

In the wake of Alexander the Great's conquests and premature death, his empire was divided among his generals.

1. Rome, Italy was 1,480 miles from Jerusalem. Damascus, Syria, was 130 miles from Jerusalem. Alexandria, Egypt was 350 miles from Jerusalem. Ephesus was 650 miles from Jerusalem, and Carthage was 1,575 miles from Jerusalem. In a world where sea-lanes and roadways were frequented, we will take leave of Judea, and follow the Messianic Jewish movement's journey in the broader Greco-Roman world.

The powerful Seleucus I Nicator eventually made Antioch, Syria, the capital of his expansive eastern Mediterranean holdings. Appreciating its strategic location and being particularly anxious to maintain a solid buffer against their Parthian rivals, in 64 B.C.E. the Roman general Pompey annexed part of an independent Syria into the expanding Roman fold, in conjunction with which he also annexed Judea. Damascus, Syria was better known to Bible readers than Antioch and was similarly brought into the Roman fold, incorporated into a league of "ten cities"—i.e., the "Decapolis."[2] Damascus' importance as a caravan city cannot be overstated. Trade routes from southern Arabia, Palmyra, Petra, and the silk routes from China all converged upon it. The commodities-saturated city markets satisfied Roman demands for eastern luxuries. But the demand for *security*—particularly against Rome's nemesis, the Parthians—was much greater, resulting in Antioch's eclipsing Damascus and eventually coming into its own as an extremely important military holding. Professor Thomas Robertson sums it up well:

> Following ill-fated endeavors in the early second century against Parthia, Rome settled for its more secure border at Antioch... making it its [principal] administrative city.[3]

2. In the year 37 C.E. Caligula transferred Damascus to Nabataean control, and the Nabataean king Aretas IV Philopatris ruled Damascus from his capital in Petra. About 106 C.E., however, Nabataean Damascus was returned to Roman control.

3. Thomas A. Robinson, *Ignatius of Antioch and the Parting of the Ways: Early Jewish-Christian Relations*, p. 14.

Because Messianic Judaism surfaced and thrived in Antioch and in other cities—scattered over the Mediterranean world, and *not* just in Judean Jewish communities—and because Messianic Judaism has a much, much longer history in those and other cities, *the Messianic Jewish movement's story needs to be reflected upon within the context of the broader Mediterranean world.* This story must be told against the backdrop of the circumstances that were imposed upon its actors in a variety of places, days, and times—in the *Levant*, particularly.[4]

Many do not know the term *Levant* today. As explained previously, this was an area just north of Israel. Medieval Italians called the region the Levant after its easterly region where the sun "rises"; the term was adopted from Italian and French into many other languages, including Turkish. Depending on which way we may wish to look at it, the Levant references (1) a geographical area at the eastern edge of the Mediterranean Sea, situated at the far eastern edge of the ancient Roman Empire, or (2) the west and southwestern edge of the ancient Mesopotamian world(s). Regardless of one's perspective, circumstances imposed themselves upon Judean inhabitants in the southern edge of the Levant, resulting in the capital city's utter demise and the concomitant displacement of its entire Jewish population, all

4. As for "Messianic"—in what is called Messianic Judaism—a Messianic Jew is here construed, both then as now, as *someone who wrestles with the question of what it means to participate in the Yeshua story, on the one hand, and with the Jewish people still, on the other.* The issue then—as now—is *not* that every Messianic Jew answers the question the same on what it actually means to be a Messianic Jew. Rather, the actual nexus, the "tie that binds" Messianic believers, is the fact that like-minded individuals can and do ask the question of what it means to participate in both worlds. With that in mind, by speaking of "Messianic Jewish experience" in antiquity, drawn here is a big circle with room made for *anyone* who cares to wrestle with questions(s) associated with what it means.

of whom soon looked elsewhere for temporary and permanent residency. Upended by the ravages of wars, Jewish survivors had no choice but to devote their energy to establishing themselves afresh elsewhere, with uncertain futures, in nearby places like the enormous city of Antioch, a midway point in the Levant between Jerusalem and Mesopotamia, and a location known to be ever ready to absorb new immigrants in order to sustain itself.

If it can be shown that so-called "Christians" in the Levant were still Jewish at heart, it can be argued that it is because *they were still living Jewish* at heart—as was the case and as we shall see. That Messianic Judaism—and *not* a post-Jewish, "Christian" Christianity—was firmly established in the Levant in the sub-Apostolic and post-Apostolic eras is evidenced in and by the so-called "Christian" literature that was produced then.

In his paper, "The Multiform Jewish Heritage of Early Christianity,"[5] Professor Robert Kraft of the University of Pennsylvania states emphatically, "Christians inherited a large bulk of Jewish material and passed it along for centuries mainly in Greek. Much of this literature seems to have *originated in Semitic linguistic dress* (Hebrew or Aramaic), and much of it is either directly or indirectly apocalyptic in thrust"—a decidedly Jewish literary genre.[6] As evidence thereof, Dr. Kraft notes how wrongly attributed literature (e.g., the Syriac *Apocalypse of Baruch* and the Ethiopic *1 Enoch*)[7] "flows" in ancient Greek, Syriac, Ethiopic, Arabic, and Armenian.[8] Mindful of this, Kraft speaks of large-

5. Appeared first in Jacob Neusner (ed.), *Christianity, Judaism and Other Greco-Roman Cults* (Leiden: Brill, 1975), pp. 174–199.

6. Italics mine; Robert Kraft, "The Multiform Jewish Heritage of Early Christianity," p. 21.

7. Ibid., p. 8.

8. Ibid., p. 6.

scale Christian "adoption of apparently Jewish materials,"[9] much of which originates in the Levant. Realizing this to be the case, Professor Wayne Meeks of Yale University spoke of "a widespread Christian *infatuation* with Judaism" in the first four centuries.[10]

"Adoption"? "Infatuation"?

Can it really be?

For years, as has been noted throughout this book, all we have heard about is abandonment!

Synergy between Jewish and Messianic Jewish appropriations of Jewish thoughts and practices for so-called Christian thoughts and practices in the Levant is well supported in a variety of primary sources. Among them, worth noting is the well known (and often misunderstood) *Gospel of Matthew*, the *Didache* (an early "Christian" instruction manual from Syria) and the *Odes of Solomon* (an early, first-century "Christian" hymnal from ancient Syria), to name but a few. These and others will be considered for the light they shed upon early Messianic Jewish experience in the Levant.

Dr. Kraft summarizes his assessment of the interrelationship between Jewish and Christian sources there, saying, "It is likely that much of what went on in Semitic speaking Judaism around the turn of the era had a significant impact on some Greek speaking Jews, especially in the main urban centers of civilization"[11]—case in point: Antioch, where "According to the Hebrews" was written, our Gospel of Matthew.

We will begin our assessment there.

---

9. Ibid., p. 11.

10. Italics mine; Wayne Meeks, *Jews and Christians in Antioch in the First Four Centuries of the Common Era* (Missoula, MT: Scholars Press, 1978), p. 32; culled from Rodney Stark, *The Rise of Christianity: A Sociologist Reconsiders History*, p. 65.

11. Ibid., p. 22.

The Gospel "According to the Hebrews"

For his part, Jerome *mistakenly* tied Matthew's Gospel to the land of Judea. The assumption is not without its merits, given how Matthew's Antiochan document (1) includes Aramaic words without translation (5:22; 6:24; 27:6) and (2) assumes knowledge of Jewish customs and evidences "forms of speech that are more typically Semitic than Greek."[12] If professors Dr. Carson, Dr. Moo, and Dr. Morris are to be believed—and most all other New Testament scholars concur—*Antioch is to be preferred for Matthew's place of origination,* based in part on the fact that, like the Antiochan faith community, the document "breathes a [very] Jewish atmosphere and yet looks upon the Gentile mission in a favorable light."[13]

This Gentile-friendliness, as Duke University Professor Stanley Hauerwas notes, is evidenced alongside Matthean themes like "the relation between the church and Israel, the continuing status of the law, [and] the significance of the Temple."[14] To these, Professor Warren Carter of the Brite Divinity School in Ft. Worth, TX, adds that Matthew's people know Torah practices like (1) Sabbath-keeping, (2) purity laws, (3) tithing, (4) oaths, all of which are interpreted by Yeshua, as per 5:17 and 22:37–39, with premiums going to justice, mercy, and faithfulness in 23:23.[15] With *knowing* being

12. D.A. Carson, Douglas Moo and Leon Morris, *An Introduction to the New Testament* (Grand Rapids: Zondervan Publishing, 1992), p. 75. On p. 79, as well, reference is made to there being "so many Jewish features."

13. Ibid., p. 75.

14. Stanley Hauerwas, *Matthew* (Grand Rapids: Brazos Press, 2006), p. 20.

15. Richard A. Horsley (ed.), *Christian Origins*, p. 156.

experiential, not just intellectual, it is important to consider that Matthew's recipients lived like Jews, as opposed to just thinking like them or being sympathetic toward them.

The ancients have noted Matthew's decidedly Jewish nature for quite some time, among them Papias,[16] Ireneus (*Adv. Haer.* 3.1.1, quoted in Eusebius in *H. E.,* 5.8.2), Tertullian (*Against Marcion.* 4.2), and Origen (quoted by Eusebius in *H. E.* 6.25.3–6), to name but a few.[17] The strident, anti-Messianic churchman Epiphanius—arguably and sadly a Jew himself! —claimed that the "Ebionites" (i.e., ancient Messianic Jews) had a Matthean text that they mutilated to manufacture their defective book called *According to the Hebrews.* Lacking that sort of vitriol, Ireneus says the early Jewish believers used a Matthew text, much as the celebrated philologist St. Jerome claims he "translated the 'Gospel According to the Hebrews' into both Greek and Latin."[18] Jerome claims that Nazarenes (i.e., ancient Messianic Jews) assisted with the translation,[19] and is known to have been grateful and polite by way of response.

With its provenance in or around Antioch and an understood postwar date in the 80s as given, the following questions arise: What can we learn about Messianic Jewish experience in Antioch (or "Christianity" in Antioch) from the Gospel that originated there? Though interested in the New Testament's Jewish roots (and Matthew's, to be sure), our particular question is concerned more with the people whom Matthew was addressing than what was actually said to them.

16. Ibid., p. 68; see also n. 12.
17. Ibid., p. 70.
18. Ibid., p. 71.
19. Ibid.

What can we learn about Matthew's people—their lives and circumstances?

In his *The Formation of Christianity in Antioch: A Social-Scientific Approach to the Separation between Judaism and Christianity*, Professor Magnus Zetterholm postulates a population of 300,000–400,000 people in Antioch at the time when Messianic Judaism was establishing a hold there.[20] Others claim a higher number. Going with his conservative appraisal, however, the city's density amounts to about 195 people per acre.[21] Considering how Calcutta has about 122 people per acre, and Mumbai 185 people per acre, Dr. Zetterholm surmises that non-elite residents in Antioch—the likes of which would have been represented by the better part of the transplanted Jewish refugees who fled the war—would have indeed been struggling to make ends meet.

Leaning upon Seneca (4/5 B.C.E.–65 C.E.), who complains about conditions in Antioch, Dr. Warren Carter adds, "Most inhabitants of Antioch lived in atrocious and cramped conditions, marked by noise, filth, squalor, garbage, [exposure to] human excrement, animals, disease, fire risk, crime, social and ethnic conflicts, malnutrition, natural disaster (especially flooding) and unstable dwellings."[22] Non-elite slaves and plebeians, as distinguished from higher-ranking senatorial and equestrian classes of people, had low life expectancies in this environment: 25–40 was the average life expectancy for males; it was much

20. Others have argued for 500,000.

21. Magnus Zetterholm, *The Formation of Christianity in Antioch: A Social-Scientific Approach to the Separation between Judaism and Christianity* (London and New York: Routledge, 2003), p. 29.

22. In his chapter "Matthew's People," found in Richard A. Horsley (ed.), *Christian Origins* (Minneapolis: Fortress Press, 2010), p. 146.

less for females. Infant mortality was particularly high, as well, at 1:5, not to mention increased deaths for the mothers laboring to bring children into their miserable world. Most did not have running water, requiring water to be brought in jugs. Urine and feces were deposited in the streets and left there.

For those living in Antioch, life came replete with many challenges.

Josephus spoke of a dense Jewish population in Antioch (*Ant.* 7.43). Professor Zetterholm estimates there were nearly 22,000 Jews in the city and approximately thirty synagogues, but knows of no distinct Jewish quarter, per se, as was the case in Sardis, Alexandria, and Rome.[23]

Jews had secured some benefits in Antioch. For example, they had already earned the cherished right to assemble as a legal *collegia*, to observe the Sabbath and other festivals, to collect and send the Temple tax to Jerusalem (something that, as noted, was appropriated for other purposes), to observe dietary laws, and to be exempted both from obligations to the imperial cult and from mandatory military service. Though Jews enjoyed a legal status, many Jews were nevertheless accused of impiety, misanthropy, and xenophobia, and seen by outsiders as "evil incarnate."[24] Jews were seen as "hard to manage." When Jewish riots broke out in Alexandria in the summer of 38 C.E., delegations had to be sent to Rome to restore Judaism's legal status. Claudius restored it, with provisions that kept Jews in check. The mandate was sent to Syria and used as a precedent in managing the Jewish population.[25]

23. Magnus Zetterholm, *The Formation of Christianity in Antioch: A Social-Scientific Approach to the Separation between Judaism and Christianity*, p. 37.

24. Ibid., p. 113.

25. Ibid., p. 116.

Josephus said Jews helped found the city of Antioch initially and had a long history in the city since inception (*Against Apion* 2.39; *Ant.* 12.119). Despite difficulties every now and again, overall, political life was reasonably tranquil for Jews in Antioch.

Waves of newcomer immigrants were forever being absorbed by Jews there, and this, of course, taxed Jewish benevolence systems that would easily be stretched too thin. The recently resettled Messianic Jews were in a particularly precarious place socially, having recently come to Antioch as refugees from the Judean wars. They, of course, would have been assisted by Messianic Jews already resident there before the wars (see below), much as they would have been helped along through the larger Jewish community's largesse. Tacitus noted, "Jews were 'extremely loyal toward one another, and always ready to show compassion'" (*Hist.* 5.5).[26] Still, challenging as the times were, issues associated with food production, distribution, and consumption would have weighed heavily upon the hearts and minds of the myriad non-elite Jewish peasants who lived in and around Antioch.

Endemic undernourishment would have prompted sickness and its evil cousin, contagion, with the resulting malnutrition making people especially prone to malaria, diarrhea, dysentery, cholera, typhus, and bacillus meningitis. Inadequate sewage and water would similarly have contributed toward swollen eyes, skin rashes, measles, mumps, scarlet fever, and smallpox. Mindful of the above, Professor Carter wonders, "Is it any wonder then that food production, distribution and trade and consumption and diet

26. Ibid., p. 127.

[stories] figure predominantly in the Gospel [of Matthew],[27] a document that was first written for Jews in Antioch and that was first embraced by them.

Let us look more closely at them—the Messianic Jews in Antioch.

Antioch's Torah-observant, Messianic Jewish community knew that Yeshua did not come to "abolish the[ir] Torah" (Matt. 5:17). Nobody in Antioch—or anywhere—ever heard him or any immediate disciple of his say he did. Those who recall the famous 2 Macc. 6–7 story of a woman who gave up her sons in defiance of the reigning powers' insistence they assimilate (cf., Heb. 11:35) should consider that the story originates in Antioch. Jews in Antioch had a proud tradition of Torah-compliance, which, to be sure, directed them to place a premium on charity, not just on dietary obligations.

As for advocating a restrictive diet, would not stricter Torah-compliance assist Jews in an environment where plague was rife—as was the case in Europe? One would think so. In any case, the premium on charity in this abysmal world is particularly noteworthy here.

Matthew's Messianic believers heard stories of "the poor" who had "the Good News preached to them" (Matt. 11:5). They learned that people mattered more than livestock (12:11–12) and that miracle provisions were to be had by the faithful (6:25–34).

Whatever Matthew says about Yeshua and Torah observance aside, stories of planting and harvesting (13:3–9, 18–24; 12:1), of vineyards (20:1–16; 21:28–32, 33–35), of day laborers (20:1–16), of fieldwork (24:40-41), of fishing (4:18–

27. Ibid., p. 157

22; 13:47–50), of trading (13:45–46), of marketplaces (11:16), as with noting food staples like fish (7:9–10), bread (15:9–10), and wine (26:26–29) most surely would have spoken the loudest and been heard by people burdened by deep-felt yearnings associated with life's menacing problems. *Nobody felt burdened by Torah observance; they all felt burdened by life.* People who "labor and are burdened" were invited to come to Yeshua for their daily necessities (11:28–30), to pray for "daily bread" (6:11) and were beckoned to not worry too much about "what we will eat and drink" (6:25–34), as seems so much the case with humans who find themselves oppressed by the turbulence of trying times.[28]

What might this document say about its recipients—the first Messianic believers who lived in the Levant?

Messianic Jews had lots to worry about.

Deficiency and contagion would have been ubiquitous for Matthew's hearers who dwelt in impoverished ghettos in first-century Antioch. Numerous summary passages to that effect are noted (4:23–25; 9:35; 11:4–5) coupled with various miracle scenes (8–9; 12:9–14, 22; 15:21–28; 17:14–20; 20:29–34), of the healing of lepers (8:1–4; 11:5), of removing blindness (9:27–31; 11:5; 12:22; 15:30-31; 20:30; 21:14), of relieving pains (4:24), and conquering various types of deformities and paralysis (4:24; 8:6; 9:2; 11:5; 12:9–14; 15:30; 21:14). These, of course, would lend a particular kind of credence to an expression often used in recent days: "Jesus is the answer for the world today."[29]

---

28. Stories told of crops threatened by aggressive and poisonous weeds (13:24–30), threatening famines (24:7), and beggars (9:27–31; 20:29–34) would have spoken about the needs of many at this time.

29. Richard A. Horsley (ed.), *Christian Origins*, p. 158.

Taking leave of today's world in preference for yesterday's in Antioch, it is worth noting that a sickened, saddened, and maddened, devilish world was found wanting by Israel's justice-oriented Messiah, and was under God's judgment for both its rank perfidy and its attendant rising misery index. Yeshua is seen helping and healing, as well as forcefully confronting and condemning the reigning spiritual/political powers in that world on behalf of Jewish people (and all people) time and time again, in 4:24; 8:16, 28, 33; 9:32; 15:22. One illustration is particularly striking and telling in that regard, especially in a first-century Jewish context.

As noted at the outset, the Roman Legion X Fretensis was stationed in Syria with a variety of other legions. The X Fretensis transferred and fought against Jerusalem in 66–70 C.E., however, and was stationed on the Temple Mount for many, many years afterward. Its mascot was a pig—an affront to Jews, to be sure. In Mark's accounting of a miracle scene, a man was possessed by a demon named "Legion" (see Mk. 5:9). In both Matthew and Mark's reckonings of his deliverance, after being excised from the unfortunate man, "Legion" entered pigs who, in turn, ran down an embankment to be finally destroyed in the Sea of Galilee (Matt. 8:28–34). Whatever else could be garnered from the story, the social implications would not have gone unnoticed by the story's Jewish hearers who would have rejoiced to see a symbol of the Legion X being destroyed by Israel's Messiah.

Explications of Yeshua's teaching, stories, and activities with Jewish eyes are promising indeed. Here, interested for the most part in the stories' recipients, and not the meaning and merits of the stories themselves, *the Gospel*—along with much else in the New Testament—*was written with the needs and interests of Messianic Jews in the Levant in mind.*

Beyond the felt needs they would have had were interests that were uniquely related to the Gospel's own needs: to expand the Messianic Kingdom into worlds and cultures beyond Judea. That Messianic Judaism in Matthew was both *cosmopolitan* and *global-oriented* is evidenced by how the baby King's arrival was said to have been celebrated by "wise men" from the nations (2:1–12), by the Kingdom's being likened to a "dragnet cast into the sea that gathered *all kinds of fish*" (13:47) and by the Kingdom's messengers being under a mandate to then "Go into *all the world*… and make disciples of *all nations*" (28:19–20), to name but a few samplings in support of the point.

To be sure, Matthew's people—and thus Messianic Jews in Syria, as a rule—were poor people living out precarious lives in a foreign land. They lived as Jewish people in that foreign land, however. No longer the dominant group in Syria as they were in Judea—even a Hellenized Judea—they developed socially as a subculture within the larger Levantine cultural milieu. It might perhaps be that, separated from a narrower Pharisaic approach to Judaism, Matthew's cosmopolitan Messianic people were very much oriented toward non-Jews. This is only to be expected; after all, *this was their world!*

The Odes of Solomon

If one grants that, in many respects, Antioch's Messianic believers found themselves oppressed, depressed, suppressed, and repressed, one might wonder how they sought to get beyond their difficult circumstances.

To help us get a window into their experience, we'll hear from Princeton Theological Seminary Professor James Charlesworth who gathered an impressive collection of scholars to work on a collection of ancient documents, some of which are said to have come from their world—Syria. The collection is called *Old Testament Pseudepigrapha*. One said to be from in or around Antioch in the first century is particularly telling and will be the object of our attention here—the *Odes of Solomon*. Dr. Sidney Griffith, referenced previously, is again insightful along with Dr. Charlesworth, particularly because he underscores how "identity was preserved in the burgeoning success of the Syriac language"[30] and with the language's notions then transmitted through *music*. If one grants the importance of music in Edessa and the Syriac world on the whole, one might be better able to appreciate what was being communicated by music in Messianic Jewish circles, particularly through the *Odes of Solomon* on which Professor Charlesworth worked.

Dr. Charlesworth attributes the *Odes* to "the earliest group of Jewish Christians"—to use his language—and grants their origination in "Edessa or one of the many Jewish Christian communities that dotted the region between Edessa and Antioch, or in Antioch-on-the-Orontes."[31]. Their importance cannot be overestimated, according to Professor Charlesworth, who goes on to say that with a "strong Jewish tone" these Syriac/Aramaic songs "preserve precious reminders of the

30. Sidney Griffith, "Christianity in Edessa and the Syriac-Speaking World: Mani, Bar Daysan and Ephraem; The Struggle for Allegiance on the Aramean Frontier" (www.sage.edu/faculty/salomd/ld/Edessa.htm), p. 4.

31. James Charlesworth, *Old Testament Pseudepigrapha*, Vol. II (Garden City: Doubleday & Company, 1985), p. 727.

first [Jewish] attempts to articulate the unparalleled experience of the advent of the Messiah."[32] They, according to him, are "so Jewish in tone and perspective that scholars from the beginning until the present have been persuaded, incorrectly, that they are *essentially Jewish*"[33]—i.e., Hebraic, but not in a Messianic Jewish sense.

Let us consider the *Odes,* in brief. Noteworthy are *Messianic Jewish descriptions of supernatural wonders and miraculous healings.* In *Ode* 6:1, for example, the songwriter says, "The Spirit of the Lord speaks through my members" and then in vv. 15–16 when noting that even "lives who were about to expire they have seized from death, and members which had fallen, they have restored and set up." The Messianic Jewish *Odes* are more explicit, yet, in 18:3: "Infirmities fled from my body, and it stood firm for the Lord by his will; because his Kingdom is firm." That there "was no sickness or affliction or suffering" in a healed body is noted in 21:4, prompting the Messianic Jewish Syrian psalmist to say, "I raised my arms on high, on account of the grace of the Lord" in v. 1. Speaking of raising, in 25:9 the Messianic Jewish psalmist says, "because your right hand raised me," it has "caused sickness to pass from me."

Transcending circumstances that are less than hoped for is aided by inspirational worship. Antiochan Messianic Jews got an "arm up" on prevailing circumstance by so doing, which gave rise to their extending their arms upward in praise to God.

In 35:7, the ancient Messianic songwriter demonstrates this when saying, "I extend my hands in the ascent of myself, and I

32. Ibid.

33. Italics mine; Ibid., p. 725.

directed myself near the Most High, and I was saved near him." This up-reaching form of praise and prayer is further described in 27:1–3, where we hear, "I extend my hands and hallowed my Lord; for the expansion of my hands is his sign; and my extension is the upright cross"[34]—a striking remembrance of the Cross. The question of who would be included in the "I," as in "I extend my hands" above is a question of no little significance—especially in Antioch.

Issues of exclusion and inclusion impose themselves upon students of early church experience, thanks in large measure to the works of Dr. Mark Nanos in his work on Romans and Galatians—contributions that are underrepresented in this paper, based on the assumption that he is reasonably well-known to modern Messianic Jews already. Were Gentiles in or out? Especially in Antioch, it seems, the question of whether Gentiles were to be fully admitted and associate with Jewish believers has been the object of much attention—since the issue was raised in the Galatians text (see above).

While consulting the commentaries and/or getting behind Nanos goes beyond the purpose of this presentation, it is worth noting here, with a treatment of the *Odes* particularly, how *inclusive* the Messianic verses were. As proof, in 10:5 the statement and implications are unmistakable: The "Gentiles who had been scattered were gathered together, but I was not defiled by my love (for them), because they had praised me in high places."

Is this not telling—and striking?

34. Praying in a manner designed to remember the Cross distinguishes these early Messianic Jews from modern ones who, because of the bad connotations associated with the Cross for Jews with the passage of time, get little utility by remembering it.

Not being "defiled" by my love for Gentiles refers to understandings and prejudices that resonated in some circles in the first centuries B.C.E. and C.E. The words are here put in the Messiah's mouth, saying, in effect, because "they praised me," I praise and accept them. "They," of course, are Jewish-friendly Gentiles, who, according to the one who wrote the psalm and those who sung it, were construed as included within the commonwealth of Israel by virtue of their association with Yeshua and the people who trusted in him.

Though life was difficult for Messianic Jews and their Gentile associates in first-century Syria (and thereafter), it seems believers got a "leg up" on it, and that they "together" worshipped a God who enabled them to have measured success, *together.*

Let us now move beyond the *Odes* to consider Messianic manuals that may well have been used along with those songs—the *Didache* and the *Didascalia.* If not the manuals themselves, certainly the ideas reflected there would have circulated, since they were the product of the Messianic communities.

The *Didache* and the *Didascalia*

Not Scripture in the classical sense, the *Didache*—known more fully as *The Didache: The Lord's Teaching Through the Twelve Apostles to the Nations* (Note: "*to the Nations*")—was a well received instruction manual that used the Scriptures (Matthew's Syrian-originated Gospel, particularly) to educate and assimilate new believers. This included Jewish members initially and presumably, in time, it applied to *non*-Jews. According to Dr. Aaron Milavec, the *Didache* "reveals more about how Jewish-Christians saw themselves and how they adapted their Judaism for Gentiles than any other book in the Christian Scriptures"[35]—not least of which is how the author(s) retained traditional Jewish understandings and practices while making room for Gentiles within their Jewish Yeshua-believing world.

Except for what many call the New Testament itself, this mid first- to early second-century document from Syria is one of the best sources to ascertain the church's earliest Christian/Messianic practices. The *Didache* gives a window into what Yeshua believers thought and felt, as well as into how they performed in the ancient world as an extension of those thoughts—what we call "praxis" today.

Associated with the "*Shema*," the "*v'ahavtah*" (i.e., to "love the Lord y/our God") opens the *Didache,* immediately after which Yeshua's "Love your neighbor as yourself" follows, and introduces a chapter that foreshadows a good swatch of Matthew's "Sermon on the Mount." (Chapter 1)[36] Prohibitions against "pedastry"—i.e., illicit, same-sex relationships between men and boys—which was both common and celebrated in Greek culture, follow in the next section, where murdering children by abandonment (practiced even then) and abortion were renounced. (Chapter 2) A list of forbidden practices follows, which include a prohibition against "omens" (common with Romans), enchanting, astrology, and idolatry, generally, with mention then of "magical arts," "witchcraft," and "murderers of children." (Chapters 3 and 5) Exhortations

---

35. Aaron Milavec, *The Didache:* Faith, Hope, and Life of the Earliest Christian Communities, 50-70 C.E. (Mahwah: Paulist Press, 2003), p. vii.

36. Rabbi Russ Resnick, Professor Brad Young, and others have been particularly intent on helping us see how the "Sermon on the Mount"—what Resnick refers to as "Torah on the Top"—is thoroughly Jewish.

toward caring and sharing follow (Chapter 4), after which special applications for non-Jewish recipients of the Messianic message are noted.

"Concerning food," matters taken up in both the Corinthian and Galatian correspondences, "bear what you are able" is the order of the day in the *Didache.* This relaxed requirement seems to place the burden on the conscience of the consumer, with no preconceived one requirement—based upon the Mosaic constitution—assumed normative for all. (Chapter 6) The author is not heard advocating for one position over another, much as he, in effect, seems to be saying, "c'est la vie," "viva la difference," or "Let your conscience be your guide."

"Concerning baptism," after noting its tripartite conduction "in the Name of the Father, Son, and Spirit," the *Didache* follows the Jewish preference for "living water"—i.e., moving water. Its place as the initial preference aside, should circumstances or preference dictate against the standard Jewish practice, "baptize in other water" is allowed, or, if there is no tub or body of water, pouring out water "three times upon the head into the Name of the Father and Son and Holy Spirit" is said to suffice. (Chapter 7) Noteworthy is the retention of the Jewish practice, with modification and moderations both noted and accepted, depending upon circumstances.

Concerning prayer and fasting, the *Didache* advocates for both, except for the fact that the days (not necessarily times) are differentiated from the norms that prevail in Judaism. Instead of Monday and Thursday, as was the habit of Jewish people, Wednesday and Friday are preferred. While one could use the text to cast aspersions upon Jewish practice, it seems best to simply note that Messianic Jewish people were differentiating from their non-Messianic associates—not condemning. Three daily prayer times are retained, however, as with Judaism. (Chapter 8)

The Passover Seder is then remembered through what is called the "Eucharist." The "bread scattered over the hills, and was gathered together and became one, so let the Church be gathered together *from the ends of the earth*" is expressed. The "ends of the earth" expression in the liturgical prayer references the fuller title of the work in question: "Didache… *to the Nations*," and likely describes the receptivity and cosmopolitanism that was first noted in Antioch and cherished thereafter by many Messianic Jewish believers. (Chapter 9–10) Messianic Jews in Antioch were open to the broader culture. Why wouldn't they be? Outside of the ancestral homeland as they were, they were hosted in and by the larger culture themselves, which, of necessity, would prompt a more open approach to the larger world.

Ascertaining true and false prophets is the object of attention in 11–13 and 15, with a premium placed on a determination of whether the ministers *do* or *do not* ask for financial support. Having a healthy work ethic is understood as preferable, with all other inclinations avoided. (Chapter 11–13 and 15)

Much as the *Didache* changed fasting and prayer days, so too the main worship day is distinguished from Judaism. "But every Lord's Day gather yourselves together…" is the word. (There is much evidence to suggest that Jewish believers gathered on the Sabbath still and added an early morning worship service in honor of Yeshua, as per the exhortation here.) It is argued that the divide between Messianic believers and non-Jewish believers was promoted by Gentile bishops who wanted to push constituents away from Sabbath observance toward Sunday worship, which, till then, had not been the abiding practice.

The *Didache* closes by pressing for eschatological watchfulness, an interest fully in accord with the fervor that was so very pronounced in Syria and supported in eschatological literature, as noted elsewhere. (Chapter 16)

Before leaving the *Didache,* a word about one of its children is in order: the *Didascalia.*

Writing for the JewishEncyclopedia.com—a contemporary source for things Jewish—Dr. Kaufmann Kohler (who took his rabbinical training under Samson Raphael Hirsch) notes how the *Didascalia,* like the older *Didache*, is "based upon an original Jewish work, transformed by extensive interpolations and slight alterations into a Christian document of great authority." This instruction manual is known more commonly by the title *Apostolic Constitutions* or by the longer title *Constitutions of the Holy Apostles [composed] by Clemens, Bishop and Citizen of Rome*. Syriac, Coptic, Ethiopic, and Arabic versions bear the shorter name *Didascalia.*

According to the late Dr. Kohler, this work is of "great value to the student of Jewish and Church history, as it contains a large amount of haggadic and halachic material derived from unknown Jewish sources, and casts a flood light upon Talmudic and New Testament literature." Touched-up by later Christian editors, the "Christian interpolator… is easily recognized," according to Kohler, "by the interruptions of the context, by ill-fitting New Testament references and by occasional outbursts of Jew-hatred in glaring contrast to the Jewish spirit of the main work."

As for the Jewish nature of the work, let it suffice that it echoes the *Didache,* employs the *Shema*, speaks of our "Holy and perfect fathers Abraham, Isaac, and Jacob," employs an older version of the "Eighteen Benedictions," refers to believers gathering "on the Day of the Lord," remembers the Ten Words (i.e., the "Decalogue"), reminds of the seventh day, month, and year, and points to the "Sabbath rest" as the seventh day of creation.

The *Pseudo-Clementine Recognitions*

The *Clementine Recognitions* have come down to us in Greek, by way of a fourth-century C.E. translation done by Tyrannius Rufinus. A partial Syriac translation embracing the *Recognitions* (books 1–3), and what is called the *Clementine Homilies* (books 10–14) is preserved in two extant manuscripts from the early fifth century. Samplings of the *Clementine Recognitions* exist in both Arabic and in Slavonic as well, revealing their widening circulation.[37] Of interest are descriptions of early believers' Jewishness, preserved in the Syriac version, which presumably would have been produced, circulated, and preserved in the Levant.

The author speaks of "*our* Hebrew nation" in Bk 1.32, *not* "their Hebrew nation"—evidence of his identification with the people of Israel. He goes on to explain that, since the Messiah's advent, sacrifices are no longer necessary, with the "invocation of His Name" being sufficient to effect a

37. I am here using Alexander Roberts and James Donaldson's edited version in the Ante-Nicene Christian Library, in *The Writings of Tatian and Theophilus, and the Clementine Recognitions* (Edinburg: T&T Clark, 1952), copied from the Harvard University Library.

remedy for sin and its consequence (1.39). This is also noted in chapter 44 where he speaks of the "abolition of sacrifices," and chapter 64 where "the time of sacrifices has now passed away." The Temple had long since been destroyed by the time of this writing, so this perspective not only fits theologically, but it fits in the world *after* Jerusalem's destruction in 70 C.E. The disciples are described as "unhurt from the destruction of war," referring to Messianic Jews' deliverance from the first war—one that, according to the *Recognitions,* "impends over the unbelieving nation"—thus seen as a form of judgment.

Miraculous deliverance with signs and wonders accompany Yeshua's ministry in 1.40, likened to Moses' in 1:41. In chapter 42 we also read, "Moses wrought signs and wonders, so also did Jesus." After extolling the similarities and expressing a belief that Yeshua is the "Eternal Messiah," the author says something that is both striking and revealing—particularly for our purposes here: "For in this point *only* does there seem to be any difference between us who believe in Jesus and the unbelieving Jews." Aside from believing in Yeshua, the author says, in effect, that the *communities are identical.* These believers lived and functioned as Jews, distinguished only by a different understanding of Yeshua's message and nature. Whatever else one may say about early believers aside, it is what they say about themselves that matters.

That noted. the author says, "the church…constituted in Jerusalem was *most plentifully multiplied* and grew, being governed with the *most righteous ordinances by James*, who was ordained bishop in it by the Lord." That the movement was flourishing among Jews counters the ludicrous notion that all Jews there flatly rejected Yeshua. Credence given to James is understood best when considered against the backdrop of his having been known to be a Torah-observant Messianic Jew—as with the rest there—and not a "converted" or ex-Jew who went on to establish a new religion. That stated, the *Clementine Recognitions* takes the matter up again in 1.50, saying, "…and *on this point only there is disagreement between us and them.* For they, themselves know and expect that the Messiah will come; but that He has come already in humility," even he who is called Yeshua, "they do not know," while we do.

How was it that non-Jews came to know him?

Cosmopolitan Messianic Judaism in Antioch

As noted, for too long now, well-intentioned individuals have promoted a Syrian-based, Pauline version of "Gentile Christianity" standing over against, and above, a spiritually lesser-grade, "legalistic," Jerusalem-based, Messianic Judaism of the original community there. This perspective needs to be revisited and to give way to a better telling of the story.

In *The Faith of the Mother Church: An Essay on the Theology of the Judeo-Christians*, Franciscan scholar Emmanuel Testa parrots this disparaging misconception when he speaks of Judeo-Christians who "swarmed" toward the shores of the Galilee, Trans-Jordan, Syria, and Asia Minor and who "were more or less fanatically attached to their own rites."[38]

Jewish affections were noted in the previous section. Leaving a consideration of the pejorative-sounding "fanatically attached" (to Jewish tradition) aside, Father Testa notes how

38. Emmanuel Testa, *The Faith of the Mother Church: An Essay on the Theology of the Judeo-Christians* (Jerusalem: Franciscan Printing Press, 1992), p. 15.

these "attached" Judeo-Christians—to use his term (and an often-used one, I might add)—continued "for centuries" to be "influential" in so-called "Christian" circles [39] beyond Judea—and in Syria. We have seen this as well.

Testa notes how the later Nicene Fathers of 325 C.E., wanting to diminish the continual influence of these "fanatical" Judeo-Christians and distinguish themselves from them, distanced themselves from "Ebionite tendencies" (i.e., Messianic Jewish tendencies) "so much so that, as the Emperor Constantine wrote on the occasion, there was [to be] nothing in common between the 'Christians' and the most inimical crowd of Jews."[40]

The agitating "Jews," of course, were principally—though not exclusively—Messianic Jews and Jewish-friendly Gentile affiliates, eventually felt to be "schismatic" by many in the later Latin church, who saw them as unfit and "cut off" from the Catholic "mother" church, and consequentially condemned for the crime of being too Jewish. We're told that "new liturgical rites replaced those archaic ones."[41] By labeling Jewish presence and practices in Yeshua-believing contexts "archaic,"[42] the new rites were seen as a providential evolution away from Jewishness, something accepted as being natural and celebrated as being good.

These matters aside, for the moment, *we should reject the notion of a Pauline, anti-Jewish, Syrian-based movement*

---

39. Ibid., p. 16.

40. Ibid; see also the encyclical as per Eusebius in *De Vita Constantini* III, 19–20.

41. Ibid., p. 17.

42. For a fuller treatment of this movement away from things Jewish, see Jeffrey Seif, *The Evolution of a Revolution: Reflections on Ancient Christianity in Its Judaistic, Hellenistic and Romanistic Expressions* (Lanham, Md: University Press of America, 1994), passim.

standing at odds with a Jewish-loving, Jerusalem-based movement. A fresh look at the New Testament, and at so-called "Christian" beginnings in Antioch, will buttress the point. As evidence, attend to the New Testament's own record of the early movement's expansion to see if it reflects Philo-Jewish or Anti-Jewish tendencies.

Taking a New Look at Christian Beginnings in Antioch

To begin, let us consider how Jews anticipated a Jewish mission to non-Jews, and is thus not a betrayal of the Jewish spirit. That noted, we will then consider the New Testament's telling of the movement's development in Acts.

Long before Messianic Jews fled to Syria and its environs in the wake of the wars—where much of early Messianic Jewish experience took place—Antioch had established itself as a center of Messianic belief and practice. For his part, Luke took pains to underscore how intrinsic a cosmopolitan, beyond-Judea world vision was for the Messianic movement headquartered in Antioch, and how this openness to others was at the very heart of the Messianic movement's constitution.

The Hebrew Bible had long envisioned a Messianic world vision and regeneration. In Isaiah, for example, one day "*all nations* flow" to the Jewish world in the end of days (italics mine; 2:2), when "many people[s] come" in v. 2 to hear "the word of the Lord from Jerusalem" in v. 3. The Hebrew notes later that "the earth will be full of the knowledge of the L-rd," in 11:9, when "the Gentiles shall seek him" in v. 10, with the result that "the Assyrian will come" to the Lord in 19:18–25—and note that Syria is arguably a shortened version of Assyria—and that Assyria and Israel will be united.

Contemporary musings aside, *1 Enoch* 10:21 spoke of a time when "all children of the people will become righteous, and all nations shall worship and bless me" as did *Tobit* 13:11 in saying "…many nations will come to You from far away… to your Holy Name." These both confirm a cosmopolitanism that existed in Jewish antiquity beyond the pale of New Testament influences.[43]

In conjunction with these Jewish visions of a religious world that opens up to Gentiles in the Messianic era is the New Testament's telling of how it was faithful to that decidedly Jewish vision.

In Acts 1:8, readers are informed that the Yeshua experience was outward bound at the heart, and from the very start, with emphasis going to its appropriation for people at the very "end[s] of the earth." Perhaps intending to delineate the contours of the Roman "earth," in 2:9–10 Luke takes readers to the Empire's edge and, beginning at its far eastern expanse and moving westward from there, notes how individuals from among the Parthians, Medes, Elamites, as well as residents of Mesopotamia, Judea, Cappadocia, Pontus, Asia, Phrygia, Pamphylia, Egypt, parts of Libya (northern Africa), Cyrene, and Rome were on hand to experience the birth of the Messianic movement in Judea.

Lucan/Pauline cosmopolitanism—over against some constituents' preference for a narrower Judean ethnocentrism—is further revealed in Acts, when disputes between Hebrew-speaking "Hebrews" and Greek-speaking "Hellenists" arose

43. This is explored by Zetterholm, in Magnus Zetterholm, *The Formation of Christianity in Antioch: A Social-Scientific Approach to the Separation between Judaism and Christianity.*

in Jerusalem in 6:1. These disagreements arose over claims that Greek Jews were being slighted in favor of Hebrews with the distribution of benevolence funds collected for all. The contentious matter was settled when the Hebraist disciples selected Jews with Greek names to superintend the benevolence monies in v. 5. Stephen is noted at the head of the servants/deacons, followed by Philip, Prochorus, Nicanor, Timon, Parmenas, and one named Nicolaus, who Luke describes as a "proselyte from *Antioch*"—and by all means *please take note of the name "Antioch."*

After Stephen's impassioned speech in 6:8–7:60 expressing fidelity to the ancestral Jewish people and religion as well as to Yeshua, who he claimed represented the best of both, he was mercilessly slaughtered. Noting both his martyrdom and Saul/Paul's association with it, Luke described how exigent circumstances further imposed themselves upon Judean believers, with the net result that many were "scattered throughout the regions of Judea and Samaria" in 8:1. Commenting later in 11:19, Luke noted that "those who were scattered because of the persecution of Stephen traveled as far as Phoenicia and Cyprus and Antioch"—with special attention once again given to a place called Antioch.

Luke picked up on this in v. 20, noting how "[Jewish] men from Cyprus and Cyrene…[came to] Antioch" and spoke to more culture-friendly "Hellenists." So successful were they, according to Luke in v. 22, that when "a report of this came to the ears of the church" (more accurately, the congregation) in Jerusalem, "they dispatched [a Jewish transplant to Jerusalem from the Mediterranean island of Cyprus named Yosef/Joseph, but also known as] Barnabas to Antioch" (4:36–37) to assist. Feeling the need for some further assistance, "Barnabas went to Tarsus to look for Saul… and brought him to Antioch" (v. 25).

Together, these Jews, neither of whom were citizens of Israel, contributed to the work in Syria for a year.

They came to Antioch, a renowned world city.

Writing in the fourth century C.E. in *Orations II*, Libanius said, "…if he sits in our marketplace he will sample every city, there will be so many people from each place." Cicero, for his part, called the cosmopolitan city of Antioch "the seat of learned men and of liberal sciences" (*Pro Archia* 3; *Pausanias, Descr* 8.33.3). Despite this elite perspective we must remember that, as Professor Robinson points out, "many [Jews] would have been slaves; many agriculturalists; many day laborers; many poor."[44]

According to Luke, it was there and then "in Antioch where the [Messianic Jewish] disciples were first called 'Christians'" (11:26). At face value, it would seem that non-Jewish "Christianity" could therefore claim to have begun in Antioch as a movement best differentiated from the first Messianic Jewish experience, *but this is a point that begs clarification and requires some clarification.*

The Antiochan Messianic "Christians" *wer*e connected to two worlds. Like non-Messianic Jews in Antioch, they endeavored to be loyal to Rome. They did not participate in the initial war in the 60s C.E., nor did they participate in the revolt against Trajan fifty years later. Still, they endeavored to maintain connections to the Jewish people in Judea—not *dis*connection—which is noted clearly in Acts 11:27–30.

44. Thomas A. Robinson, *Ignatius of Antioch and the Parting of the Ways: Early Jewish-Christian Relations* (Peabody: Hendrickson, 2009), p. 23.

Reports of a coming "famine" under Claudius (41–54 C.E.) galvanized the newly minted "Christians" and the "disciples determined, everyone according to his ability, to send relief to the brothers [and sisters] living in Judea" (v. 29).

A filial bond is noted between the so-called Christians in Antioch and the believers in Judea, is it not? The believers in Antioch are represented as a Judea-loving group.

Beyond sending one-time relief monies, it seems that the eclectic association of believers in the birthplace of "Christianity" were devoted as well to sending emissaries. As evidence, in 13:1–4, Luke describes a cosmopolitan group of leaders made up of (1) a Jew from Cyprus named Barnabas, (2) one Simeon called "Niger" (i.e., meaning "black"[45]), (3) a northern African from Cyrene named Lucius, (4) a wealthy brother more directly connected to Israel named Manaen, and (5) Saul. This group singled out Josef/Barnabas and Saul/Paul and sent them westward where they garnered speaking engagements in synagogues in every city they entered.

Much as the Gospel traveled to Antioch through Jews, those who went forth from Antioch followed the tradition and took the Gospel to Jews.

In 13:5, the emissaries/apostles from Antioch "proclaimed the Word of God in the synagogues" in Cyprus. Sailing north to Perga then, in the midsection of Anatolia and to Antioch of Pisidia, the troop did the same. They "went into the synagogue" there, in v. 14, after which Paul was beckoned to stand up and offer a word in vv. 15–47. Synagogue participation was their

45. Though Romans were big on "class," discrimination based on race was an affront to Roman sensibilities. That being the case, I don't construe the designation "black" as anything other than a friendly description. One in the group is noted as an islander, another a rich man, etc.

custom—*not* simply a missionary strategy—as is evidenced throughout and noted emphatically in 17:1–3 where Luke says "Paul went in [to the synagogue(s)] as was his custom." Luke testifies in 13:48 how *Jewish-loving "Gentiles" in synagogues were particularly encouraged by Paul's message.* After ministering in Antioch of Pisidia, Paul went to Iconium where the entourage similarly "entered together into the Jewish synagogue… and a great number of both *Jews and Greeks* believed" (Italics mine; 14:1ff).

After ministering later in Lystra and Derbe (in Laconia), the team went to Lystra, where rabble-rousers from Antioch of Pisidia and Iconium caused them no little grief (vv. 19–24). Not the least bit dissuaded, the Messianic emissaries pressed through and pressed on, eventually making their way back to "Antioch, where they had [first] been commended to the Grace of G-d for the work" (vv. 24–26).

While back in Antioch, following their first journey, Luke reports that some extremist Messianic Jews from Jerusalem came and unsettled Paul by advocating that non-Jewish constituents needed to adhere more closely to the requirements handed down by Mosaic law—e.g., circumcision (15:1–21). Not the least bit kindly disposed toward the message or the messengers, Paul believed that circumcision wasn't mandatory for Gentiles and wanted redress for the grievances caused by the messengers from Jerusalem. Paul, Barnabas, and others went to Jerusalem where a gathering was convened to sort through Torah-related issues.

Paul and his company returned to Antioch victorious with a favorable judgment literally in hand saying that Yeshua followers "[need] not trouble those of the Gentiles" (v. 19) with the requirements of Mosaic law and addressed specifically to "Gentiles in Antioch and Syria and Cilicia" (v. 23). They "remained in Antioch, teaching and preaching the Word of the L-rd" (v. 35). Luke mentions Antioch once more in passing, noting how Paul stopped there in 18:22–23 in the wake of his second journey.

In conjunction with Luke's testimony, Paul went on record to inform constituents in Galatia of a spirited contest he had with Peter (known as Cephas) in Antioch.

"When Cephas came to Antioch," said Paul, "I opposed him to his face, because he stood condemned" (Gal. 2:11). By catering to some who pressed Jewish believers to distance themselves from Gentile associations at the dinner table (2:12), a vacillating Peter was found wanting in Paul's eyes. Charging that Peter was "acting hypocritically" and being "led astray" (v. 13), Paul demanded in v. 14 "… [H]ow can you force the Gentiles to live like Jews?"

While circumcision, dietary issues, table customs, and other matters relating to Jewish and Gentile believers' commitment to the ancestral Jewish religion are worthy of exploring in their own right, the main purpose in raising them here is to underscore how Antioch was an important administrative center for the Jewish Yeshua-believing community during the Apostolic era—as well as in the sub-Apostolic and post-Apostolic eras later.

Antioch served as the Messianic movement's northern headquarters, more than a mere "road stop" or temporary ministry outpost. Therefore, what happened there and was modeled there was deemed important. Beyond noting this, Bible readers are again advised to pause when considering the supposed difference between Antioch's "Christians" and Jerusalem's "Messianic Jews." They, in effect, were one and the same, *separated more by geography than philosophy*—except for an apparent friendliness toward the broader, non-Jewish culture.

In any case, it is obvious that the term "Christian" was *not* invented to differentiate the Syrian "Christian" believers in Antioch from the Messianic Jews in Judea. Professor Warren Carter put it succinctly: "They had not separated from the people and heritage of Israel, but still identified themselves as part of the large Judean population resident within Antioch."[46] Seeing themselves as belonging to the tradition of Israel and Israel's God,[47] believers in Antioch functioned as a group "*within* Judaism," where they "followed Israel's traditions and practices as interpreted by Jesus."[48]

This was their problem according to Franciscan scholar Immanuel Testa (noted previously) who, wanting to be gracious, said, "The reasons for the friction [between Messianic Jews and differentiated Gentile Christians] must be sought in the breakdown of unity, communion and ritual more than in doctrinal deviations." According to him, "the Judeo-Christians were a simple people, guilty only of having attached to old ways, archaic projects, and to a theological vocabulary considered outdated by the ethno-Christian faithful."[49] This is a perspective, and everyone is entitled to

46. See Richard A. Horsley (ed.), *Christian Origins* (Minneapolis: Fortress Press, 2010), p. 138.

47. Ibid., p. 139.

48. Ibid.

49. Emmanuel Testa, *The Faith of the Mother Church: An Essay on the Theology of the Judeo-Christians*, p. 18.

one. Personally, however, *this author is not sure if they were guilty of anything at all.*

Beyond Jewish believers' acknowledgement and fidelity to the ancestral religion—or should one say, *in conjunction with it*—worth noting is their appreciation for non-Jewish acknowledgement. "For when He came," says the *Clementine Recognitions,* "He was not at all acknowledged by those who seemed to expect Him…; whereas those who had heard nothing at all of Him, both believe that He has come, and hope that He is to come." To whom are the *Recognitions* referring? To Gentiles, obviously. Bemoaning the lack of a total or wide acceptance of Yeshua by Jewish people, in chapter 61 we read, "… 'that He assumed a Jewish body, and was born among the Jews, how has not this incited us all to love Him?'" The last is a reasonable question. It is worth asking along with it: *How is it that those who did embrace him more fully disdained the people who brought him to them—the Jews?* To investigate that question while maintaining a focus on Levantine experiences, we will now consider Gentile attraction, disdain, and ambivalence. After that, we will continue to track the Messianic movement's penetration in the Mediterranean world.

Chapter 5

Pro-Judaic and Anti-Judaic Tendencies in the Ancient Roman World

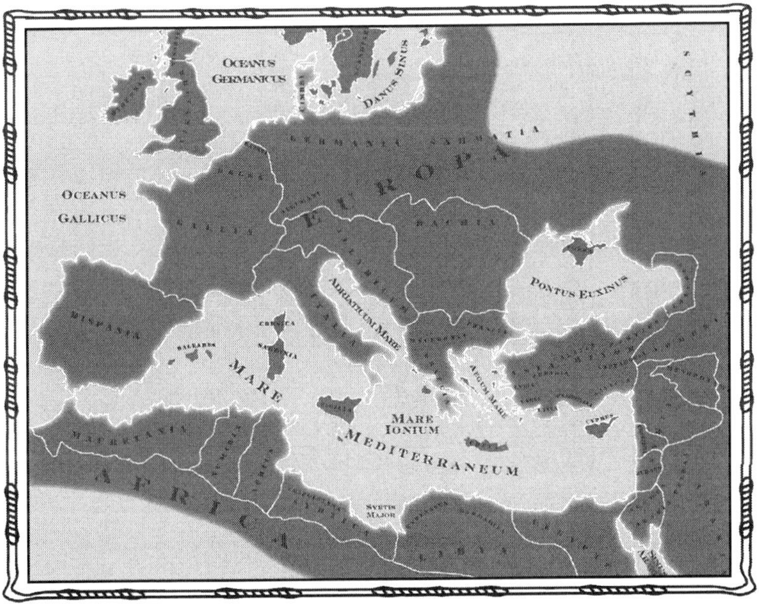

Introduction

The samplings in the previous chapters barely scratch the surface of positive Jewish influences described in Christian literature in and from the Levant—influences that were felt for many, many years to come. Vestiges of Jewish imprints are found everywhere in Christianity's essential and historical literature and have resonated within those documents for centuries. This prevalence can be attributed in part to the fact that many non-Jews were attracted to, and influenced by, Jewish people, Jewish religion, and Jewish culture—both *before* and *after* they were exposed to a particularly Messianic Jewish form of Judaism. The infatuation with things Jewish was noted by the ancients, as was disdain for things Jewish.

Pro-Judaic Tendencies in the Ancient Roman World

The term "Philo-Judaism" refers to individuals who love Judaism. Quite a few Gentiles could be thus designated as evidenced by Josephus, who observed how many Gentiles "adopted Jewish customs and manners" (*War* 2.463) and that Jews were "constantly attracting to their religious ceremonies multitudes of Greeks" (*Wars* 7.45). Elsewhere he said, perhaps not in hyperbolic fashion, that there "is not one [single] city, Greek or barbarian, to which our [Jewish] customs… have not spread" (*Against Apion* 2.282). Particularly, "… [in] the whole of Syria… each city has its Judaizers" (*War* 2.262–63).

What "Judaizers" meant was raised previously and will be considered in some detail later. Flavius Josephus explains that "in Damascus [Syria] men noted how 'wives had all become subject to the Jewish religion'" (*War* 2.559–60). There surely is some overstatement in the implication that *all* wives were coming over to Judaism; still the point is clear—as is the chagrin: Judaism was popular enough to draw such hyperbolic scorn. (Later, we will explore precisely why it was that non-Jewish women were attracted to Judaism, and then Messianic Judaism.) For his part, Dio Cassius said Jews were "converting many of the natives to their [Jewish] ways" (*Roman History* 57.18.5a). Tacitus similarly spoke of "those who come over to [the Jewish] religion" (*Histories* 5.5). Lending even more credence to Jewish attractiveness, and speaking perhaps in a disparaging manner with regard to it, Horace said, "we, like Jews, will compel you to join our throng" (*Satires* 1.4.142–143).

Epigraphic evidence in Asia and Rome speaks of "proselytes"[1] in higher echelons who appreciated the Jewish world and ways. "Veturia Paula," for example, was remembered as "a proselyte for 16 years under the name of Sarah, mother [or patroness] of the synagogues of Campus and Voluminus." Julia Severa, a patroness of the Jewish community, was known to have financed a synagogue in Phrygia. (Her son, L. Servenius Cornutus, served in the Senate under Nero in 73 C.E. and was legate to the proconsul in Asia. Another relative, L. Iulius Severus, served as a consul.)

According to Josephus, other Jewish-friendly friends in high Roman places included Emperor Nero's mistress Poppaea Sabina who "pleaded on behalf of the Jews." Titus, the elder son of Vespasian—both of whom participated in the sack of Jerusalem—took a Jewish woman named Bernice as his mistress with him back to Rome after the war, which would give him a Jewish-friendly voice in the bedroom at the very least. Lastly in this regard, Professor Magnus Zetterholm, in *The Formation of Christianity in Antioch*, alights upon Judaism's presence and influence in culture by referencing St. Augustine in *Civ.* 6.11, citing Seneca who exclaimed, "the customs of the accursed [Jewish] race have gained such influence that they are now received. The vanquished have given laws to the victors."[2]

1. Ibid., p. 13.
2. Magnus Zetterholm, *The Formation of Christianity in Antioch* (London: Routledge, 2003), p. 127.

Issues associated with calling Jews an "accursed race" were briefly considered above and are considered below. That the disparagement was not ubiquitous is evidenced, perhaps, by the fact that the largest area in the Jerusalem Temple's environs was the "Court of the Gentiles"—and the largest by far, mind you! This is telling, as it underscores how untold numbers of Gentiles were attracted to Jewish culture. Were that not the case, why the big court to remember and/or accommodate them?

Speaking of "largest," and looking just south of the "Court of the Gentiles" to the "City of David," one could not help but notice the largest facility there, one that handily protruded in the city's first-century C.E. skyline. Built in the style of the Parthian Empire—an architectural feature very much in vogue in the Levant—was the Adiabene Royal Palace(s). Josephus noted this in *War* 5.352–353 and 6.356. Visitors to Jerusalem today, who happen upon the 1:50 scale model of the old city, are similarly drawn to the palace situated just next to David's old residence in the city that bears his name. The palace takes a full half of the hill of the City of David. It was brought to life in modernity by archeologist Dr. Mikhael Avi-Yonah's reconstruction, which is used in the model of the old city.

Architectural refabrications aside, noteworthy here is the fact that the palace was built by Queen Helene of Adiabene who, with her sons, converted to Judaism in 36 C.E. and took residence in Jerusalem. The name "Adiabene" is derived from the Syria-Aramaic *Hady'ab* or *Hday'ad* and references an ancient kingdom nestled between Mesopotamia's Tigris River, just to the east of Syria at the edge of the Levant.

Referring to stories of famous conversions to Judaism, Dr. Thomas A. Robinson, professor of Religious Studies at the University of Lethbridge in Alberta, Canada, comments in *Ignatius of Antioch and the Parting of the Ways: Early Jewish-Christian Relations,* "Two of the most famous Jews of the second century, the translator Aquila and the rabbi Tarphon (or Tarfon) were proselytes [to Judaism]; Aquila moved from paganism to Christianity [so called] but finally converted to Judaism about the time of Ignatius."[3] More will be said about Ignatius—and heard from Dr. Robinson—in a moment; let it suffice here to simply note the obvious: Judaism had a considerable amount of street appeal.

Why did many Gentiles find Judaism—and then Messianic Judaism—attractive? Many who examined Roman religious sensibilities found them wanting. This will be considered in more detail later. Here, a word or two about Roman religion is in order, simply to note why many Gentiles would view Judaism—and then Messianic Judaism—as a more inspirational alternative.[4]

Romans had concerns about this life and the afterlife.[5] Believing people could placate the divines and secure benefits for themselves that way, many ancient Romans were given to frequenting temples where they brought offerings. Greek

---

3. Thomas A. Robinson, *Ignatius of Antioch and the Parting of the Ways: Early Jewish-Christian Relations* (Peabody: Hendrickson, 2009), pp. 65–66.

4. For an excellent and fuller accounting, see Everett Ferguson, *Backgrounds of Early Christianity*, 2nd ed. (Grand Rapids: Eerdmans Publishing, 1993).

5. A proper burial was considered very important, for example, lest the deceased Roman wander perpetually in a phantasmal, ghost-like state of unrest, never being afforded the peace granted to the dead who had been properly interred. The *Iliad* opened with souls being thrust into Hades, which was depicted as a dreary place where, according to Homer, life continued but in a manner not worth living. How might one avoid this dreaded nonexistence? Roman religious tradition was deemed important, owing to a belief that it could purchase safe passage to the next world, much as it could enhance the passage through this one.

and then Roman temples had treasury rooms to hold the gifts offered to the deities in the interest of securing their approval on Olympus and their consequent favors on Earth beneath. The faithful came bearing gifts; many wanted a gift in return—a sign from the gods, an omen, or an oracle.[6] Something to help—a touch from heaven.

Superstitious as many were, accessing heaven's powers in some form was deemed important. So prominent was this type of religious activity that cities were known to send official delegations to the sacred shrines to inquire of the divinities' prophets on matters of economics, war, and politics, as well as to address official religious matters.

Just a few miles west of Antioch was an extremely famous park, in the midst of which was a massive temple dedicated to the Pythian Apollo, and home to a statue of the god who was adored in Antioch. Though there were a variety of different "daughter" sanctuaries in the ancient Roman world, pride of place was given to the religious "mother house" at Delphi—considered to have been Zeus' main spot and the actual "center of the earth." It was at this site that Apollo, the quintessential Greek male and warrior, once killed the "Python"—a spectacular she-serpent deemed sacred to a certain earth goddess in early Minoan civilization. For this reason, the heroic and idealized Apollo factored significantly at Delphi—as in Antioch, later—where he was perceived as Zeus' personal representative. It was at Delphi where Apollo is said to have become the actual god of prophecy and the official spokesman for Zeus. A priestess seemed to have been the main

6. Collins noted that "in general, they were consulted in serious crises of any kind" (Ibid., p. 320).

feature at the shrines, however, where she presided over the main religious attraction there, that of oracle giving.

Romans solicited the services of celibate priestesses at shrines. Forgoing sexual activity was construed as a prerequisite to the religious service of uttering the prophetic words. At the temple, a female priestess-prophetess, a "pythia," would go into a trance-like state from which she would allegedly utter the words of the gods. In such a state, she would be consulted by inquirers who lined up to have an audience with her as they sought heavenly help with their earthly concerns.

Romans reached upward and inquired of their gods. Jewish-friendly Romans were less inclined to do so, being more disposed to seek the God of Israel. This created no small stir as is amply described in the classical sources.

Anti-Judaic Tendencies in the Ancient Roman World

As noted previously, Jews had problems in the Roman world. Jews had problems before, during, and immediately after the New Testament era. Valerius Maximus wrote that Cornelius Hispanus, along with all Chaldaic and Asiatic astrologers from the Levant, expelled all Jews from Rome. Within one hundred years during the time of Cicero, however, many Jews made their way back. Though tolerated by Augustus and others, the Jewish religion appeared absurd to many and its practitioners seen as antisocial. Tacitus said Jews were persecuted because of their "hatred of the human race," a perception held by many because of their refusal to participate in public activities dedicated to the Romans' patrons and patron gods. Though Jews were granted an official waiver on the grounds of the religion's monotheistic foundation, their unwillingness to do obeisance to the gods, or to the emperor as a semi-divine, was viewed by Romans as a form of "atheism" and gross "impiety." Their exemptions from military service exacerbated the problem. With this in mind, Professor Magnus Zetterholm observes that the "[affront] to the official polis religion…[was] an act of impiety that could result in exile or even death."[7]

The Roman satirist Juvenal voiced the sentiments of others when he construed Judaism as a "barbaric superstition" (*Satires* 14.96–106), with its mutilations (circumcision), dietary restrictions, and more. Jews were the object of private scorn and public derision. Under Tiberius, Caligula, and initially under Claudius, Jews were able to make some advances, though. However, official toleration ended with Caesar Claudius' edict in 49 C.E. calling for the expulsion of Jews from Rome—something Luke notes in Acts 18:2. By the time Nero came to power in 54 C.E., the anti-Jewish measures were rescinded, owing perhaps to Seneca's positive influence in his administration—at least at first.[8]

Endeavoring, no doubt, to escape negative stigmas associated with being Jewish, Josephus tells how the son of the Jews' chief magistrate in Antioch publicly denounced "his own father and other Jews, accusing them of a design to burn the whole city to the ground in one night." He also, Josephus reports, is said to have "delivered up some foreign Jews as accomplices to the plot" (*War* 7.46–47). Adding further

7. Magnus Zetterholm, *The Formation of Christianity in Antioch* (London: Routledge, 2003), p. 27.

8. See Wolfgang Wiefel, "The Jewish Community in Ancient Rome and the Origins of Roman Christianity," in Karl Donfried (ed.) *The Romans Debate* (Peabody: Hendrickson Publishers, 1991), pp. 85–101.

religious insults to these injuries, in 52–53 C.E., the chief magistrate's son endeavored to prevent Jews from celebrating the Sabbath.[9] There is an argument that he was an ambitious Roman military officer, particularly bent on showing his fidelity to the reigning power over and against his own kin to facilitate his advancement. (Who knows?) That Jews distanced themselves from their own and assimilated into Roman culture is evidenced by Philo of Alexandria's Jewish nephew, Tiberius Julius Alexander, who was appointed procurator of Judea in 46 C.E. and then governor of Egypt in 66 C.E. He was responsible for the suppression of the Jewish uprising in Alexandria.[10]

Anti-Judaic Tendencies in Levantine Christian Worlds

As noted above, difficulties notwithstanding, Judaism was deemed attractive by many and drew no small amount of attention—*both negative and positive.* On the basis of the salience of its virtues (over and against Roman mysticism and utilitarianism) and the beauty of those endeavoring to live following Torah, the Jewish religion stood out as a moral beacon in an essentially virtueless and spiritually rudderless world.

Luke is referred to by Eusebius as "by race an Antiochian," and is thus said to have come from Antioch (*Ecc. Hist.* 3.4.6). Time and time again, Luke notes that Paul's *Gentile converts were themselves half-baked Jews* whom Paul ("The Apostle to the Gentiles") met in synagogues when he traveled about. These first fruits were not garden-variety, everyday Romans he just happened to have met on the streets. No, Paul's "Gentiles" were Judaism-lovers—people he met in the

9. Ibid., p. 76.
10. Ibid.

synagogues he frequented. Though many of Paul's first fruits knew of Judaism beforehand, many new Gentile believers had their first exposure to Judaism through their associations with Messianic/"Christian" communities.

The Jewish forms and features in the early "Christian" faith and practices invoked the ire of *non*-Jewish-friendly Levantine church leaders, prompting them to eventually call for a parting of the ways. To cite one example here, the *Epistle of Barnabas* was written between 100–150 C.E. at a place and time when Judaism was apparently exerting considerable influence in and around the Levant and upon non-Jewish Christians—likely in either Alexandria or Syria, or both. Written to help Christians "not be shipwrecked by conversion to their law,"[11] an obvious premium was placed on insisting that Christians avoid fasting, circumcision, food laws, and the Sabbath.[12] The writer hoped to ensure that they *not* "rush forward as rash acceptors of their [Jewish] laws" [13] (*Barn.* 3.8) and thus take refuge in a religious Jewish world that has long since been "abandoned," according to the anti-Messianic church leaders (*Barn.* 4.7).

Sometimes it is good to listen closely to critics for what they uncover about those they criticize. In this case, the pressure

11. Michele Murray, *Playing A Jewish Game: Gentile Christian Judaizing in the First and Second Centuries C.E.* (Waterloo: Wilfrid Laurier University Press, 2004), pp. 47–48. Dr. Murray's text is the source for many of the extracts from Scripture noted here to underscore the point.

12. Ibid., p. 50.

13. Speaking with regard to the Sabbath, for example, in *Barnabas* 15 the author postulates: "…concerning the Sabbath in the Decalogue… Attend my children to the meaning of this expression: 'He finished in six days'… and then 'six days, that is six thousand years, all things will be finished…' This can only be construed as meaning: 'when his Son comes [again]' then the rest will be fulfilled. For now, however, applicable are the texts against its literal keeping, which read: 'Your new moons and Sabbaths I cannot endure' and 'your present Sabbaths are not acceptable to me.'"

to avoid fasting, circumcision, dietary restrictions, and the Sabbath reveals that many *early Levantine "Christian"/ Messianic Jews lived within the parameters of a Jewish worldview and culture.*

Commenting on the *Epistle of Barnabas*, the editors of the *Ante-Nicean Father*s note a dated and jaded vantage point: "…the old Judaizing, which St. Paul had anathematized and confuted… assert[ed] itself again" and prompted the writing of so-called *Barnaba*s to refute it. "It is interesting as a specimen of their conflict with a *persistent [form of] Judaism* which St. Paul had defeated and anathematized, but which was *cropping out among believers*."[14] This, of course, is a dated perspective—one in need of adjustment, to put it mildly. Instead of it "surfacing again," the better reading of the situation is that it never left. In any case, the spirit behind the translators' antiquated perspectives was then further corroborated by Professor Adolf Hilgenfeld, who says the *Epistle of Barnabas* was written "at the close of the first century" and "with the view of *winning [people] back, or guarding [some] from, a Judaic form of Christianity*."[15]

First and arguably foremost among those seeking to guard against so-called "Judaizing tendencies," was the famous bishop Ignatius of Antioch. The third bishop of Antioch and a disciple of the Apostle John, according to Eusebius, Ignatius was martyred in the eleventh year of Trajan, or 108 C.E. Condemned to die for reasons unknown to us, Ignatius was transported from Antioch to Rome to meet his fate. Undaunted

14. Italics mine. A. Cleveland Coxe (ed.)., *The Apostolic Fathers*, Vol. 1 (Grand Rapids: Wm. B. Eerdmans Publishing, 1979), p. 133.
15. Italics mine. Ibid., p. 135.

and in fact encouraged by the prospect of giving his life for Christ, as he put it, the intrepid bishop used his final trip to pass on final words—in the form of half a dozen letters to various churches in Asia Minor. Of these, statements written to the Magnesians and the Philadephians are particularly noteworthy for our purposes here.

Readers are encouraged to pause, take note, and prepare to be disconcerted by what Ignatius wrote, but to avoid jumping to conclusions about what he seems to be saying, however. A careful examination of the texts will provide perspective that will alleviate some initial objections—at least to some extent.

In *Magn.* 10:3, Ignatius said:

> It is monstrous to talk of Jesus Christ and to practice Judaism.

In *Phld.* 6:1, he further argued:

> If anyone interpret Judaism to you do not listen to him; for it is better to hear Christianity from the circumcised than Judaism from the uncircumcised.

The language of the first passage is forceful, as is the second—and, on both counts, quite telling. Judaism had been in Antioch for 400 years before Ignatius. Against that backdrop, how can it be that within 100 years of Yeshua's death, and thus after Messianic Judaism had been in Antioch for seventy years, we are hearing calls to separate Yeshua and his followers from his historical people, culture, and religion?

Seeing an amalgamation of "Jesus Christ" and the "practice of Judaism" as "monstrous" is indeed troubling, is it not? Exhorting people to refuse those who "interpret Judaism" a hearing, similarly, underscores a troubling devaluation of Jewish experience, as is the bishop's advice to disdain it. In *Phld.* 6:1–2, Judaism was further demonized, describing it as "tombstones and sepulchers of the dead," not to mention associating it with "the wicked arts and snares of the prince of this world." In *Magn.* 8:1–2 Ignatius stated his position succinctly: "…if we are living until now according to Judaism, we confess that we have not received grace."

Ignatius employs the term "Christian" seventeen times, mostly in *contrast* to "Judaism."[16] The differentiation is obvious. The seeming disdain is apparent. The reasons for both are *not.* What is going on here? Why is it happening? What might this reveal about Messianic Jewish experience in the Levant?

Professor Thomas Robinson surmises that Ignatius' "Judaizers… [are still] members of his [Christian] community" in Antioch,[17] and that they "were meeting on the Sabbath for their separate eucharists," whereas Ignatius' church appears to have conducted its corporate religious life primarily on Sundays.[18] If he is correct, and there is good reason to think he is, then here is yet more evidence of the accord between "Christianity" in Antioch and Messianic Judaism, as it would seem that they were still intertwined. "Many [Gentiles]," says Robinson, "would have had their first substantial exposure

16. Thomas A. Robinson, *Ignatius of Antioch and the Parting of the Ways: Early Jewish-Christian Relations*, p. 88.

17. Ibid., p. 99.

18. Ibid., p. 104.

to elements of Judaism from within their new [Christian] environment,"[19] which would have made them "curious."[20] In sum, Dr. Robinson believes that *Ignatius' "Judaizing" opponents were "Gentiles who converted to Christianity but were attracted to elements of Judaism*, beyond that sanctioned by Ignatius."[21]

In conjunction with the "*denarii duo Judarorum*"—the tax previously noted—up until Domitian, Suetonius said the tax should be collected with the "utmost vigor" from all Jews, even the nonobservant Jews. That it was to be collected from "those who *without* publicly acknowledging that faith yet lived as Jews"[22] has struck some as interesting. What does he mean by people "living as Jews" *without* really being Jews? He could well be talking about Messianic Gentiles.

In 67.14.1–2, Dio Cassius notes that "Domitian… slew along with many others, Flavius Clemens, the consul… and [his wife] Flavia Domitilla," both relatives of the emperor, because they "drifted into Jewish ways."[23] What did "drifting into Jewish ways" mean? Did they become Messianic Jewish Gentiles? After Domitian's assassination in 96 C.E., his successor Nerva adopted a more Jewish-friendly disposition. Dio Cassius reported, "Nerva said… no persons were permitted to accuse anybody of adopting the Jewish mode of life" (68.1.2). Should "adopting a Jewish mode of life," which was *legal*, be distinguished from that

19. Ibid., p. 111.
20. Ibid., p. 110.
21. Italics mine; Ibid., p. 117.
22. Magnus Zetterholm, *The Formation of Christianity in Antioch: A Social-Scientific Approach to the Separation between Judaism and Christianity*, p. 186–187.
23. Ibid., p. 187.

adopted by Gentile believers in Yeshua? By virtue of their affections for both Jewish and Gentile communities, they were *deprived of legal status as Jews or Gentiles*, and could thus be construed as simply adopting a "mode." There is an argument that they should.

Speaking of Gentile Christian affections for things Jewish, the lauded Jewish scholar Dr. Shaye J. D. Cohen, the Littauer Professor of Hebrew Literature and Philosophy in the Department of Near Eastern Languages and Civilizations of Harvard University, weighs in similarly: "In both *Philadelphians* and *Magnesians* the 'Judaism' that arouses Ignatius' attention and anger is within the church. *The Judaism is the 'Judaism' of Christians within the Christian community*, not the 'Judaism' of Jews 'out there' beyond it."[24] According to Dr. Cohen, the anger was directed toward a formidable proclivity in Levantine Christianity—Gentile believers' affection for Jewish and Messianic experience.

While granting Professor Cohen's point, in both a personal conversation and a follow-up correspondence, Dr. Mark Kinzer—a man whom I consider to be one of the most thoughtful theologians in the modern-day Messianic Jewish revival—responded, "I certainly agree that the focus of Ignatius is on Jews and Jewish practice in the Church, rather than Jews and Jewish practice outside the Church. However, when he says in Magnesians 10, 'Put aside then the evil leaven (*kakein zumein*), which has grown old and sour, and turn to the new leaven, which is Jesus Christ' and then says 'It is monstrous to talk of Jesus Christ and to practice Judaism,' I think we can only conclude that he sees Judaism as a whole as 'evil' or

24. Italics mine; Ibid., p. 224.

'bad' leaven." If this perspective prevails, Professor Shaye J. D. Cohen's appraisal may be overly simplistic.

Ignatius is not here to straighten the modern theologians out or to cast his vote on who has the closest assessment of his position. Neither is Dio Cassius—nor most of the people noted in this volume, for that matter. Here I can do little more than note the sources, expose readers to some of the conversation generated by them, and leave readers to make tentative judgments about what they think they are hearing and seeing.

Returning to Dio Cassius' point, since Judaism was a legally sanctioned religion in the Empire, one might wonder to whom he is referring when he speaks of individuals "accused of adopting a Jewish mode of life." Had Gentiles adopted Judaism, that would have been no crime then—except in the mind's eye of Ignatius and those who agreed with him. If Gentiles adopted it, in some sense, but were not received by local non-Messianic Jewish gatekeeper authorities and thus would not have been legally considered as Jews in the Romans' eyes, these fake Jews—adjudged so by Roman standards, that is—would have been in a particularly precarious place, with no political protection in the *culture* or in the *synagogue*. Is he referring to grafted-in Messianic Gentiles, or just Jewish-friendly Gentiles?

In *Playing a Jewish Game: Gentile Christian Judaizing in the First and Second Centuries* c.e., Michele Murray, professor of Early Christian Studies at Bishop's University, weighs in on Cohen's side of the argument: "the need to ridicule Jewish observance perhaps derives from its being *too closely intertwined with Christian behavior and identity*."[25] As evidence of Judaism's influence in Antioch (and elsewhere)—and well over 200 years later—she elsewhere notes that, as late as 386/387 C.E.—and, mind you, this is over 200 years removed from Ignatius—some of Bishop John Chrysostom's congregants in Antioch "attended synagogues [on the Sabbath] and observed certain Jewish rituals including circumcision, dietary laws and rites of purification."[26] With Dr. Murray, I am inclined to believe that the tension reflects Jewish connections that were adjudged too close for comfort.

This confirms a Messianic Jewish presence and power. Was Messianic Jewish influence localized or was it widespread?

25. Italics mine; Ibid., p. 54.

26. Michele Murray, *Playing A Jewish Game: Gentile Christian Judaizing in the First and Second Centuries C.E.*, p. 43.

CHAPTER 6

JEWISH AND CHRISTIAN CONTACTS AND INFLUENCES IN EUROPE

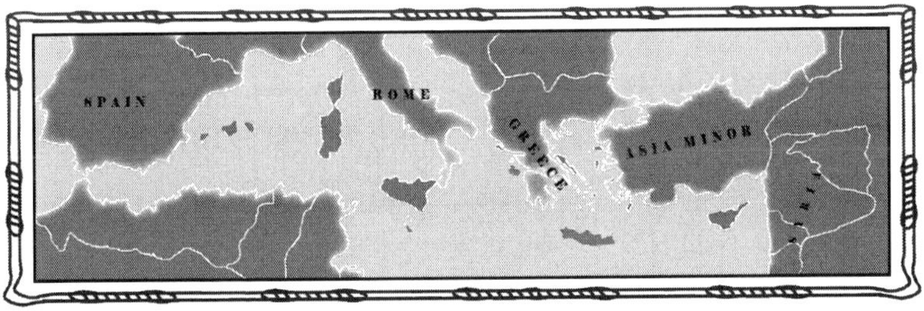

Syria, Asia Minor, Greece, Rome, and Spain

In what are called the Acts of the Apostles, the Apostles are mentioned as a group only once in passing (cf. Acts 1:15–26). The truth is, in Acts, pride of place is really given to the acts of one particular apostle—*not all.* Initially Peter gets the spotlight. He fades away rather quickly in the narrative, however, after which the real object of Luke's attention surfaces—offering an accounting of the life, travels, and teachings of an honorary "apostle," the Messianic movement's principal congregational planter and its most enduring theologian, Rabbi Saul (called Paul). A review of his travels to and through Asia Minor (Turkey), Greece, and Italy are deemed helpful here, as they give a doorway into the movement's penetration in Europe.

As noted at the outset, Paul, more so than Yeshua, is credited with beginning the religion known as "Christianity." Whatever else he was, Yeshua was a Torah-observant Jew. Though a Pharisee at the start, as noted, Paul is misconstrued as denigrating Torah observance in favor of a life devoid of the law and centered on Christ-based spirituality. Though held out to be the progenitor of the new religion, a careful reading of the primary sources leads to other conclusions. To assess the sources, we turn to Paul's biographer, Luke.

In Acts 9:32–35, Luke develops the document's and movement's outward-bound theme first noted in 1:8, and then in 11:19–30, where readers are informed how the Yeshua movement expanded into Antioch—as noted above—"where the disciples were first called Christians" (11:26). Luke then draws attention to more precarious social and economic affairs in Jerusalem and notes how the fledgling "Christian" faith community in Antioch marshaled material resources to assist those in Jerusalem (11:27–29). The financial resources were then sent to Jerusalem "by the hands of Barnabas and Saul" in v. 30. After describing the rising misery in Judea in 12:1–23, Luke gives a progress report, saying "But the word of God grew and multiplied" (v. 24), and follows with a description of Barnabas and Paul's return to Antioch from Jerusalem with John Mark in tow at the time (v. 25).

The first Christians intended to help Jews in Judea, did they not?

One might wonder where that spirit is today. That aside, their fidelity to the Messianic movement in Judea is further noted.

The outward-bound, forward-thrusting missionary spirit is said to have gotten the better of the congregation in Antioch (13:1–2), with the result that Paul and Barnabas were selected and dispatched to serve as the Antioch Messianic movement's official advocates in Asia Minor (v. 3). Luke gives an abbreviated telling of their first circuit tour in Asia Minor (modern Islamic Turkey) in 13–14, but interestingly, he spends more time detailing a follow-up conference in Acts 15 regarding misunderstandings over the nature of Paul's ministry.

Problems arising in conjunction with Paul's unconventional Gentile mission needed addressing. After a rather engaging Messianic leadership conference in vv. 1–21, characterized by misunderstanding and spirited dispute over Paul's bold initiatives, Paul's Jewish-friendly *and* Gentile-friendly disposition was officially affirmed in 22–24. This noted, Luke says in v. 5 that "the churches were strengthened in the faith and increased in number daily." He then says that Paul went off again to confidently advance the Messianic Kingdom beyond Israel's borders in 6–22—with unswerving and unbounded zeal for the task. His enthusiasm was, no doubt, facilitated by the affirmation he had received in Jerusalem from the brethren there who affirmed the legitimacy of his open-minded approach to those of non-Jewish background.

Believing himself under a Divine mandate to press on with his egalitarian and cosmopolitan vision, one that made room for Jews and Gentiles to be together in the Messiah, in vv. 9–10 readers are told that Paul opted to forgo his overland travels in and around Asia Minor and press westward to Greece by sea. Though a bit discouraged by constantly-closing doors there, he sailed from Troas in v. 11 and eventually made his way to Philippi in v. 12, where the Jews in Greece granted him speaking privileges—as was usually the case when he traveled about.

The biblical narrative reports that Paul frequented synagogues everywhere he went, engaging Jews there, as well as scores of *Jewish-loving Gentiles*. The "Apostle to the Gentiles" should perhaps better be called the "Apostle to the *Jewish-Loving* Gentiles" on the basis that all his Gentiles converts were individuals he met in synagogues as he traveled about. (See 17:1ff)

That aside, for now, once on the Greek mainland, Paul made his way west by southwest to Amphipolis, Apollonia, Thessalonica, Berea, and elsewhere in 17:1ff. After going to synagogues in Macedonia (northern Greece) and establishing a presence for the Messianic movement along the northern and eastern sides of Greece, the intrepid apostolic explorer ventured further southward down the Grecian peninsula to Athens in southern Greece (v. 15). After an unproductive stint there (with no synagogue to frequent), he eventually made his way to the sizable Jewish community in Corinth (18:1ff). His second journey's conclusion was then noted in vv. 19–22 where Paul was said to have departed that region for his home base in Antioch (v. 22).

Paul is forever observed frequenting synagogues, is he not?

After a season of refreshment in Antioch, Paul took off again in 18:23, on what scholars call his "Third Missionary Journey." Attention is given to events in Ephesus in 19:1–41 where a riot is said to have ensued. It was provoked by chagrined idol-makers upset by a drop in revenue associated with the Messianic Jewish movement's growth. Amid the turbulence of it all, God's grace was manifest still. Difficulties aside, Luke gives another progress report, saying, "the word of the Lord grew mightily and prevailed" (v. 20). When "the uproar had ceased," Paul then departed for Greece again (20:1–2).

Paul conducted and completed his third journey and then went to Jerusalem with an enormous offering in hand which he had collected for the Jewish believers there. Anxious, no doubt, to demonstrate his fidelity to the people and place, he'd hoped that the generous offering would help endear the Jerusalem-based Messianic movement to the movement in Greece composed of Jews and non-Jews. He was not given a hearing, however. A riot ensued, and he was then arrested in Jerusalem and held on bogus charges (21:17–32). From there, he went to Caesarea (by sea) where he was confined (vv. 33–32), after which he was sent to Rome for trial per his direct appeal (22:27–28).

Paul is observed making his way around the Greco-Roman world, where he frequents synagogues and tells of the life and teachings of Yeshua. He advocates for a community of Jews and Gentiles together. He makes friends and enemies in the process. After chronicling a variety of journeys, Luke describes how Paul went to Rome to answer for his conduct. Luke then takes leave of his chronicle, but not before noting Paul's intransigence as a preacher/teacher while under "house arrest" in the imperial city. Luke does not tell us what became of Paul at all. He finishes with Paul telling Jewish rabbis in Rome that he himself always was and forever will be a Torah-observant Jew—period. Luke concludes the book telling of Paul's acts and affairs with a final progress report—his seventh. Here he notes that the Word was still going forth unhindered in 28:30–31, saying that "Paul dwelt two whole years in his own rented house [in Rome], and received all who came to him, preaching the kingdom of God and teaching the things which concern the Lord Jesus Christ with all confidence, no one forbidding him."

With Paul in Rome, we will consider the Gospel's advancement there in more detail—and along Jewish lines.

Rome

In *Diaspora: Jews amid Greeks and Romans*, Dr. Erich S. Gruen, professor emeritus in the Department of History, University of California, says the population of Rome "exploded" in the first and second centuries B.C.E., resulting in "Jewish communities...in the late Republic and early Principate, with modern estimates of a Jewish population ranging from 20,000–60,000"[1] people.

Luke tells why and how Paul made it to Rome at that time. But what of the other Jews? Where did they come from? Why did they come?

Like our prisoner Paul, the first Jews who settled in the district of Trastevere, Rome were said to have originally been prisoners of a sort—prisoners of war, particularly, or people who were enslaved and then liberated. Some others seem to have been free men who came because of the social and commercial allure of the imperial city.

---

1. Erich S. Gruen, *Diaspora: Jews amidst Greeks and Romans* (Cambridge: Harvard University Press, 2002), p. 15.

Valerius Maximus reported in 139 B.C.E. that Jews invoked the ire of Romans and that Cornelius Hispanus/Hispalus (see above) had them expelled from Rome, for "peddling their ancient wisdom" and "for attempting to transfer their sacred rites to the Romans" (*Val. Max.* 1.3.3)[2] (Luke is explicit in noting how Paul was "peddling his wisdom," is he not?) Seneca is on record describing Jews as a most pernicious people (*sceleratissma gens*). Because he nowhere else speaks directly of Jews in his vast writings—except in this extract culled from St. Augustine's *City of God*—one cannot say that Seneca was particularly obsessed with Jews and given to slandering them. The satirist Juvenal took on Jews for adherence to dietary laws, Sabbath, circumcision, and the like, but construed the practices to be "more laughable than dangerous."[3] For his part, Tacitus was tolerant of Jews, but "angrier at the converts than at the Jews… who have deserted their native gods, ancestral traditions, homeland and families."[4] He noted, as well, that Jews had a passion for reproduction—a matter that will be considered below. After calling for and assessing Gentile views of Jews, in his section "The Jews of Rome," Professor Gruen concludes:

> Romans in the private sphere had little reason to trouble themselves over the Jews. Writers scoffed and laughed. The weird ways of the Jews provided a source of amusement, even amazement. However, they did not lead to bile, and they did not provoke hostilities. The

2. Ibid., p. 16 and n. 7 on p. 260.
3. Ibid., p. 45.
4. Ibid., pp. 46–47.

> preserved comments, even in the aftermath of the [Jewish] Revolt, convey mockery rather than malignancy.[5]

Though anti-Jewish statements appear in the Roman press, every now and again, Dr. Gruen doesn't make too much of it—and rightly so.

At the street level, however, it could be argued that Jewish ideas made headway and naturally invoked the ire of some. Why Judaism, and then Messianic Judaism, was attractive in far-away Rome was considered previously. This is a good time to press the matter further and note how in antiquity Roman women were increasingly attracted to Judaism and its daughter religion—Messianic Judaism.

"The early church was so especially attractive to [non-Jewish] women," says Professor Rodney Stark, "that in 370 [C.E.] the emperor Valentinian issued a written order to Pope Damascus I requiring that Christian missionaries cease calling on the homes of pagan women."[6] For reasons that will be unpacked below, Dr. Stark believes "women enjoyed far higher status" in Jewish and Messianic Jewish homes and communities, in Rome as elsewhere, "than did women in the Greco-Roman world at large."[7] This higher status and better

---

5. Ibid., p. 53.

6. Rodney Stark, *The Rise of Christianity: A Sociologist Reconsiders History,* p. 95. He is the principal source for this section, a considerable part of which was culled from his "The Role of Women in Christian Growth."

7. Ibid. Stark leans upon Robin Lane Fox, *Pagans and Christians* (New York: Knopf, 1987); Henry Chadwick, *The Early Church* (Harmondsworth, Middlesex: Penguin Books, 1967); Adolf von Harnack, *The Mission and Expansion of Christianity in the First Three Centuries.* Translated by John Moffatt. 2 Volumes (New York: G. P. Putnam's Sons, 1908).

treatment drew non-Jewish women into the Jewish fold and into the Messianic movement's ranks.

Writing around 200 c.e. in *The Roman History: The Reign of Augustus,* the Roman historian Dio Cassius noted there was an "extreme shortage of females" in Roman culture. Dr. J. C. Russell concurred and, for his part, posited that there were 131 males for every 100 females in the city of Rome, and 140 males for every 100 in Italy.

Why the disparity in numbers?

As we shall see, and contrary to habits among Jewish men, the disparity in numbers existed because non-Jewish Roman men tended to disrespect Roman women.

In his *The Ancient World: Manners and Morals,* Dr. Jack Lindsay noted how even in large and reasonably wealthy families "more than one daughter was practically never reared."[8] Why not? This diminished number of Roman women, according to Dr. Stark, can only be attributed to some engineering of human life, or of "tampering" with it, as Dr. Lindsay put it. With no offense to culture and morals, many, many baby girls were left to die at birth in Greco-Roman culture—as were males with deformities. Undesired baby girls were left to die at dumps at the edge of Roman cities. Most did; some, however, were picked up and raised as prostitutes.

Seneca saw the disregarding of unwanted children as "reasonable" and "commonplace."[9] Plato and Aristotle

8. Jack Lindsay, *The Ancient World: Manners and Morals* (New York: G. P. Putnam's Sons, 1968), p. 168. Of 600 families with inscriptions left in Delphi, only six reported raising more than one daughter—thus only 1%. Astounding! Troubling, is it not?

9. Rodney Stark, *The Rise of Christianity: A Sociologist Reconsiders History,* p. 118.

recommended infanticide as a legitimate state policy and lent their credence to the pagan practice as a result. Torah-minded Jews disdained the murderous practice and were quick to criticize it.

In *The Histories* 5.5, Tacitus construed the Jewish notion that it is "a deadly sin to kill an unwanted child" as one of the Jews' "sinister and revolting" ways of thinking.[10] Testifying to the horrific pagan views while positioning Jewish practice over and against them, Josephus noted, "The [Jewish] law, moreover, enjoins us to bring up our offspring, and forbids women to cause abortion or to destroy it afterward; and if a woman appears to have done so, she will be a murderer of her child." Torah forbids the murderous brazen disregard for life in the Ten Commandments. In his *Sentences of Pseudo-Phocylides,* an Alexandrian Jew similarly advised, "a woman should not… throw it [i.e. her newborn baby] before dogs and vultures of prey." In his *First Apology*, Justin Martyr expressed this sentiment with "it is wicked to expose even newly-born children… [for] we would then be murderers."[11]

Regarding the difference between pagan practices and the stance of Torah-bound Jews, Dr. Rodney Stark surmised, "the views of family… sustained by Christians revealed the Jewish origins of the movement... [those views] being "very family oriented"[12] at the core.

Messianic believers refused to condone female infanticide. Coupled with Judaism and Messianic Judaism's

10. Ibid., p. 118.

11. Ibid.

12. Ibid., p. 124.

stalwart disparagement of divorce, marital infidelity, fornication, and polygamy, it is not hard to understand how non-Jewish women could and would become attracted to Judaism. Life loving, loving, and nurturing were accentuated. Fidelity without divorce was held out to be the norm in the Jewish counter-culture and was expected of every Messianic adherent as well.[13]

Not only that, believers' marriages were entered into on better terms than what tended to prevail in the broader culture. The fortunate Roman girls who made it past the disgraceful abandonment were typically married off to older men before puberty. In his "The Age of Roman Girls at Marriage," in *Population Studies*, Dr. Keith Hopkins writes, "Romans gave their girls in marriage when they were twelve years old, or even younger," something Plutarch said caused "the hatred and fear of girls forced [into sexual relations] contrary to nature."[14] Dio Cassius said much the same, that "Girls are considered… to have reached marriageable age by their twelfth year."[15] According to Dr. Hopkins, 10 percent of pagan girls were married by age 10, with 44 percent marrying by age 14, most often with men much older and with the unions consummated at once, despite the tender age of the girls.

Women in Messiah-believing communities tended to marry later.

Though not particularly respected in the broader Greco-Roman culture, babies, girls, and older women arguably fared much, much better in the Messianic Jewish subculture.

13. Ibid., p. 104.
14. Ibid., p. 107.
15. Ibid., p. 106.

Not only were believing men more predisposed to value their marriage partners with exhortations in the Scriptures to "love their wives," but, should women fall upon hard times when untimely death claimed their husbands, the Messianic community had a responsibility to assist the unfortunate widows—their "sisters" in a communal sense. This refers to James' noting that to assist widows represents religion that is "pure and undefiled before God," and thus at its best.

The lesson was not lost to the ancients. This is revealed in Eusebius' writings, where Cornelius, Bishop of Rome, wrote to Fabius, the Bishop of Antioch, in 251 C.E. and said more than 1,500 widows and distressed persons were in the care of the local congregation, which may well have numbered about 30,000 by the time of that writing.

Arguably, the valuation of female life in Jewish communities as compared to the devaluation of female life that prevailed in the reigning culture prompted not a few women to cast their approving gazes toward the Yeshua movement. Quite a few came from the upper as well as lower classes.

In *The Body and Society: Men, Women and Sexual Renunciation in Early Christianity,* Dr. Peter Brown observed how "'women were prominent' among upper-class Christians."[16] That women were prominently represented in the believing community's ranks—way in excess of the women that presented in the broader culture where they were outnumbered 140:100 in Italy—created an unanticipated "surplus of women" in the Messianic movement at a time when the world was accustomed to a "vast surplus of men."[17]

16. Ibid., p. 99.
17. Ibid., p. 101.

This created something of a problem—as you can imagine.

In about 200 C.E., Callistus, Bishop of Rome, "upset many of his fellow clerics when he 'ruled that Christian women could live in just concubinage,' without entering into marriage"[18]—what we would call fornication. Why would a bishop provide a mechanism for such things? Professor Harnack explains that these "circumstances arose from the... problem[s] facing upper-class women whose only marital options within the Christian community were to men of far inferior rank" and that "high born women would have lost many legal privileges and [the] control of their wealth."[19] Wanting to provide a means for this growing inventory of women to secure the personal benefits of believing marriage without imposing the legal obligations of marriage that would reduce their standing, the bishop opted for another arrangement. No matter what one thinks of his position or the women, a Torah-based culture was gaining headway in a morally bankrupt world.

Dr. Stephen Spence posited, "Jewish features underlie a large part of the Roman Church." This, according to him, is "explained by its proximity and familiarity with Jewish traditions, which lead some to believe that Christianity in Rome began within the well-established Roman Jewish community."[20]

Though the notion that Roman Christianity evolved from a Jewish matrix may appear novel at first (especially

18. Ibid., p. 111.

19. Ibid., p. 112.

20. Stephanie Binder, "Jewish-Christian Contacts in the Second and Third Centuries, C.E.?" The Case of Carthage; Tertullian and the Mishnah's Views on Idolatry," in Dan Jaffee (ed.), *Studies in Rabbinic Judaism and Early Christianity: Text and Context*, p. 220.

for those inclined to think of the Roman Catholic Church as the original), a careful consideration of the sources supports the thesis *that ancient Roman Christianity came by way of Judaism and Messianic Judaism*, given the appeal of the egalitarian and redemptive natures of the respective Jewish movements.

Jewish culture was virtue-rich; pagan culture operated with a virtue deficit. Greco-Roman utilitarianism humbled and dehumanized human beings—even the citizens of the Empire. Reducing non-citizens of lesser race, class, and gender to less-than-hoped-for lives, the doomed unfortunates were socialized into accepting their unfortunate lot. Many knew they were little more than fodder to be used and abused in the gladiatorial games, to be harvested as slave-stock for the mines and agriculture, and used as human chattel to serve the various needs and interests of oppressive overlords.

Though this dehumanization tended to prevail in the larger culture on quite a grand scale, a Torah-based subculture within the reigning culture cast a loftier moral vision, where *all people*—irrespective of their race, class, or gender—had inalienable, God-given dignity and rights. That these "rights" extended to women in the decidedly patriarchal culture may well account for why women from all classes were attracted to the synagogue originally, and then why many women preferred Judaism's daughter religion as it got a foothold in ancient Rome.

Much as Christian life was impacted by Jewish life, so too was Christian death.

In *The Jews in Late Ancient Rome: Evidence of Cultural Interaction in the Roman Diaspora*, Professor Leonard Victor

Rutgers concludes that Jews and Christians shared much in common.[21] A careful assessment of archeological findings in ancient Rome and Venosa similarly prompted Professor Eric Meyers to note in his "Report on the Excavations at the Venosa Catacombs" that "Jewish and Christian burials reflect an *interdependence* and [a] closely related community of Jews and Christians in which *clear marks of demarcation were blurred* until the third and fourth centuries, C.E."[22] With this in mind, Dr. Rodney Stark goes on to quote Dr. Meyers again—it was "only when a triumphant Christianity began, late in the fourth century, to pour money into Palestine for church building and shrines, was there any serious rupture with Jews."[23]

Interesting thought, is it not?

In a subsequent volume, Professor Meyers teamed up with Professor James F. Strange and produced a book with an odd-sounding, semi-Jewish title—one noted previously: *Archeology, the Rabbis & Early Christianity*. Writing in a section entitled "Evidences of Early Christianity: Churches in the Holy Land," they revisit a misconception in need of serious rethinking: "It has long been a truism in the study of early Christianity… that Christianity sprang full-grown from the head of Constantine in the fourth century."[24] Not true, of course. That stated, the authors remind their readers that the so-called "Christian movement did not develop a fixed repertoire

21. Leonard Victor Rutgers, *The Jews in Late Ancient Rome: Evidence of Cultural Interaction in the Roman Diaspora*, pp. 260-268.

22. Italics mine; Eric M. Meyes. 1983. "Report on the Excavations at the Venosa Catacombs 1981." *Vetera Christianorum* 20:455–459; culled from Rodney Stark, *The Rise of Christianity: A Sociologist Reconsiders History*, p. 69.

23. Ibid., p. 68.

24. Eric Meyers and James F. Strange, *Archeology, the Rabbis & Early Christianity* (Nashville: Abingdon Press, 1981), p. 125.

of symbols, iconography, architecture and cultic paraphernalia until well past the first century, some would say well into the fourth."[25] Absent that, *modes of living, learning, and dying tended to remain within the Jewish milieu, from which both the people and movement began.*

This all changed, however, in Rome—as elsewhere throughout the Empire.

Writing in *The End of Ancient Christianity*, Professor Robert Markus (former member of the Institute for Advanced Studies at Princeton University and Distinguished Visiting Professor of Early Christian Studies at the Catholic University of America) evidenced the church's eventual forgetfulness of its Jewish heritage and its deliberate preference for employing pagan images and institutions in the telling of its story.

By St. Augustine's time, for example, most—but certainly not *all*—had long since disposed of Jewish ways and means, along with the employment of the Jewish calendar and worship cycle, to celebrate sacred Christian moments. Removing and/or re-appropriating some of the Church's Jewish elements were easy; the problem of what to do with pagan influences was a bit more challenging.

Professor Markus describes how Faustus once taunted St. Augustine because "Christians celebrated Kalends and solstices just as do the heathen."[26] The celebration of the "Day of the Sun" on December 25th was but one example of the Christian appropriation of pagan ritual. It, according to Dr.

25. Ibid.

26. Robert Markus, *The End of Ancient Christianity* (Cambridge: Cambridge University Press, 1991), p. 102.

Markus, was retooled and, by a "re-interpretation in a Christian context,"[27] became the world's much-beloved "Christmas." The pagans' New Year's holiday on January 1 was similarly dusted off, reinterpreted, and given its own place in Christian time and space alongside Christmas.

The famous bishop of Hippo, St. Augustine—who ministered in Carthage for a season (see below)—said, "he will lament over Christians who fill the churches on the festivals of Jerusalem, and the theatres on the festivals of Babylon."[28]

Displeased by this infatuation for the celebration of Jewish traditions (that Christians would "fill the churches on the festival of Jerusalem"), Augustine was eager to encourage people to come to the "finest show on earth," that of the "celebration of the blessed martyrs" in and through the institutional church. St. Augustine's disciple Quodvultdeus seems to have summed up his interests quite well in *Sermo* 3.2 by saying "let them 'divert their passion for spectacles.'"[29] .

"The public celebrations" developed by church leaders, says Professor Markus, "had served to articulate a public consensus and legitimated a mixed community's limited, but none the less important, urban value system." Aided by it, the clergy were eventually able to "reestablish their authority over the citizen [civic] body and recreate a civic census on a new, and now Christian, basis"[30]—and *not* a Jewish one, as had been the case.

27. Ibid., p. 103.
28. Ibid., pp. 117–118.
29. Ibid., p. 118.
30. Ibid., pp. 118–119.

With the passage of time, and owing to circumstance, the Yeshua movement lost sight of its Jewish origins. It evolved away from earlier forms and features and morphed into the non-Jewish religion it is known as today.

Spain

A brief assessment of the biblical record gives us an interesting window into this distant and majestic Mediterranean land, known today as the Iberian Peninsula. In what follows, note will be given to Spain's referencing in the biblical text, a brief consideration of how Jews came to Spain and then how ancient church leaders were bent on facilitating a divide between Jews and Christians in Spain.

In Genesis 10:4, one known as Tarshish (from whom come the Spaniards) is said to be descended from Javan (the progenitor of the Greek peoples in the isles), through Noah's son Japheth (v. 2). "From these," Moses says, "the coastland peoples of the Gentiles were separated" in v. 6. The Tarshish-Spain connection is corroborated in 1 Chron. 1:1–7, and further developed elsewhere in the Hebrew Bible. In the biblical narrative, Judean contact with distant Iberia is shown by the significant ancient trade arrangements between the Israelites, the Phoenicians headquartered in Tyre/Lebanon, and the Spaniards in distant Tarshish. In Ezekiel 27:12, for example, the prophet notes that "Tarshish did business…out of the abundance of your great wealth." Also in I Kings 10:22 we read: "For the king had a fleet of ships of Tarshish at sea with the fleet of Hiram [of Tyre]. Once every three years, the fleet of ships of Tarshish used to come bringing gold, silver, ivory, apes, and peacocks"—exotic animals and materials, to be sure.[31] Representing the westernmost expanse of the known Mediterranean world of the time, Tarshish is mentioned twice in Jonah 1:3 as the prophet's runaway place, a hideout construed as being at the end of the known world.

Construed as being at the "ends of the world" as it was, Paul's desire to go there is perfectly consistent with what we know about the intrepid explorer in Acts, and not just from his expressed intentions in his letter to the Romans.

Substantial evidence of a Jewish presence in Spain comes from the Romans. In *Facta et dicta memorabilia*, Valerius Maximus makes reference to Jews being expelled from Rome in 139 B.C.E. Hispania came under Roman control with the fall of Carthage after the Second Punic War (218–202 B.C.E.). Exactly how soon after Jews made their way there is a matter of some speculation. Some may well have gone there under the

31. Tartessus is the portion of Spain known to the Hebrews in Psalm 72:10 as "The kings of Tarshish ... kings of Sheba." Tarshish was famed for various metals exported to Tyre; most of them were drawn from Spain and Portugal, tin possibly from Cornwall or from Lusitania or Portugal. "Ships of Tarshish" are mentioned often: Psalm 48:7, "Thou brakest the ships of Tarshish with an east wind," alluding with undesigned coincidence to the event recorded in 2 Chronicles 20:36–37; "Jehoshaphat joined himself with Ahaziah king of Israel to make ships to go to Tarshish ... in Ezion Gaber ... because ... the Lord hath broken thy works," i.e., wrecked the ships. The ships of Tarshish built at Ezion Geber on the Elanitic gulf of the Red Sea (1 Kings 22:48) were intended by Jehoshaphat to trade with Africa and India; but a copyist in 2 Chronicles 20:36 makes them go to Tarshish. It is possible they were carried across the land to the Mediterranean, but more likely that "ships of Tarshish" means large vessels, as our phrase "East Indiamen" does not imply the destination but the size; the copyist mistook the phrase for the destination. So in 1 Kings 9:26, 1 Kings 10:22, and 2 Chronicles 9:21, the "peacocks" point to India for southern Asia, and the isles of the eastern archipelago are their native home. The names too are of Sanskrit etymology, *tukki*, related to Tamil *Iota*, "the tailed bird," i.e., peacock. So "apes," kaph, is related to Sanskrit *kapi*. The Greeks received the peacock from Persia, as the Greek *taos* is the Persian *tans*. Strabo makes the Boetis or Guadalquivir (great stream) be called Tartessus. An island, a town, and a region bore the name. (www.studylight.org › Dictionaries › Fausset's Bible Dictionary)

Romans as free men in order to take advantage of the land's rich resources; others, perhaps 80,000, were enslaved by the Romans under Vespasian and Titus and transported to the west during the Jewish-Roman War, after the Roman defeat and sack of Jerusalem in 70 C.E.

When in Corinth in 56–57 C.E., and while on his third missionary journey, Paul wrote a now-famous letter to the Romans in which he was very explicit about his intentions to visit Spain after finishing his business in Jerusalem (15:24, 28). Given Paul's premium of traveling where he could frequent synagogues, it can be assumed that there was a Jewish community in Spain, too. Herod's banishment to Spain by Caesar in 39 C.E. (*Wars*, 2.9.6) lends credence to the proposition, as does the fact that *Midrash Rabbah*, Leviticus 29.2, has Jews returning from Spain by 165 C.E.. Spain is mentioned in Obadiah 1:20 where we read of "the exiled of Jerusalem who are in Sepharad." *Targum Yehonathan* translates "Sepharad" as "Aspamiah" meaning "Spain." The Jewish sage Rashi concurred, as did Rabbi Abraham Iben Ezra, Radak (Rabbi David Kimchi), and Abarbanel, who went so far as to say that whole settlements in Spain were founded by exiles from Jerusalem which included prestigious families.[32]

Beyond these proofs of Jewish presence, Christian reports are found in several decrees of the Council of Elvira. Convened in the early fourth century, the council *forbade marriage between Jews and Christians in Spain.* That the church fathers felt it necessary to prohibit early Christians—perhaps Messianic Jews or at least Messianic Gentile sympathizers—from marrying Jews is rather telling. *The need to firmly press*

32. britam.org/**spain**.html.

for a disconnect likely meant that there were connections—to the chagrin of non-Jewish church leaders.[33]

When all is said and done, little substantial evidence is presented here compared with what I suspect is yet to be discovered about the Jewish experience in Spain. It is a slowly emerging story. To be sure, more work needs to be done to recover the story of Messianic Judaism in pre-Catholic Spain.

33. Ibid.; "The edicts of the Council of Elvira, although early (and perhaps precedent-setting) examples of Church-inspired anti-Semitism, provide evidence of Jews who were integrated enough into the greater community to cause alarm among some: Of the Council's 80 canonic decisions, all which pertain to Jews served to maintain a separation between the two communities (Laeuchli, pp. 75–76). It seems that by this time, the presence of Jews was of greater concern to Catholic authorities than the presence of pagans; Canon 16, which prohibited marriage with Jews, was worded more strongly than canon 15, which prohibited marriage with pagans. Canon 78 threatens those who commit adultery with Jews with ostracism. Canons 48 and 50 forbade the blessing of Christian crops by Jews and the sharing of meals with Jews, respectively."

Chapter 7

Jewish and Christian Contacts and Influences in North Africa

Jewish experience in North Africa is lost to moderns—as is ancient Messianic Jewish experience on the whole. Difficulties with reconstruction notwithstanding, we will explore extant sources and briefly consider Jewish peoples and communities in North Africa to see what we can learn about Messianic Judaism among those ancient peoples and communities. Taking leave of exotic Spain, we will cross the Mediterranean Sea and take a look at the famous North African city of Carthage. From there, we will move to the east and to Cyrene, after which we will draw closer to the biblical homeland of Judea (where our story began) by visiting ancient Alexandria, Egypt—and thus complete our introductory sweep across North Africa and our loop around the ancient Roman world.

Readers will hear modern scholars lamenting the lack of primary source material—the stuff of which historical writing is made. Though the "sands of time" have ways of covering lost cities, fresh winds and circumstance have ways of uncovering them and revealing secrets in their own time—as students of the Dead Sea Scrolls are aware. Instead of simply waiting for new discoveries to come, however, I will here rely on some of what we do know now—or what we think we know. To ascertain how the Gospel first moved down Jewish tracks in North Africa, to and through Jewish communities, we will explore how interrelationships between Jews, Jewish believers in Yeshua, and non-Jewish believers continued for generations till Jews were "depopulated" in North Africa.

Jews and Messianic Jews in Carthage

Dr. Stephanie Binder of the Department of Classical Studies at Bar-Ilan University, Israel, brings strong Jewish connections to bear on ancient North African Christian experience. In her post-Trajan, postwar "Jewish-Christian[1] Contacts in the Second and Third Centuries, C.E.?," Professor Binder took up the matter of Jewish and so-called "Christian" interactions in African antiquity.[2] She was particularly concerned with whether ancient Christians and Jews were "either different and

1. Meaning Jewish *and* Christian contacts as opposed to Jewish-Christian individuals, a term often employed when referring to Jewish people who believe in Yeshua.

2. Stephanie Binder, "Jewish-Christian Contacts in the Second and Third Centuries, C.E.?" The Case of Carthage; Tertullian and the Mishnah's Views on Idolatry," in Dan Jaffee (ed.), *Studies in Rabbinic Judaism and Early Christianity: Text and Context* (Leiden/Boston: Brill, 2010), pp. 187–230. This is the primary source for the arguments noted below, from which the others' voices were extracted.

isolated from each other or similar and intermingled, in the late second and early third centuries C.E.," in Carthage and elsewhere.[3] Her assessment of both the principal sources and the scholarly discussions on those sources yield an affirmative "yes"—that indeed *the Jewish and so-called "Christian" communities were much more connected than disconnected.*

After referencing Dr. Timothy Barnes who says, "no one really knows how Christianity came to North Africa,"[4] Dr. Binder notes others, like Dr. Rene Braun, who suspects that *Christianity came to North Africa through the Jewish community.*[5] After observing through Dr. J. C. Fredouille that the "African church seems closer to the East than the Occident"[6] (i.e., the "West"), and Dr. J. B. Rives who says, "African liturgy is more like that of the East than that of Rome"[7] and Dr. W. H. C. Frend who notes that "Christianity surely arrived through the Jewish community and from Eastern influences,"[8] she then offers her reasons for reasonable connections based on how the North African church leader Tertullian's thought processes follow Judaism's *Mishnah Avodah Zarah*, on matters of festivals (pp. 197–202), immorality and idolatry (pp. 202–203), baths (pp. 203–204), games (pp. 204–206),

3. Ibid., p. 187.

4. T. D. Barnes, *Tertullian* (Oxford: Clarendon Press, 1985), p. 68.

5. As per R. Braun, *Approaches de Tertullian: vingt-six etudes sur l'auteur et sur l'oeuvre* (Paris: Institut d'etudes augustiniennes, 1992), p. 2.

6. J. C. Fredouille, *Tertullian et la conversion de la culture antique* (Paris: Etudes augustiniennes, 1972), p. 271.

7. J. B. Rives, *Religion and Authority in Roman Carthage from Augustus to Constantine* (Oxford: Clarendon Press, 1995), p. 225.

8. W. H. C. Frend, *The Rise of Christianity* (Philadelphia: Fortress Press, 1984), p. 348 and "A Note on Tertullian and the Jews," in *Studies Patrista* 10 (1970), p. 292.

garments (p. 206), saying the names of pagan gods (pp. 206–208), schoolmasters and teachers (pp. 209–210), swearing by the names of pagan gods (pp. 210-212), outsmarting the Law (pp. 212–216), and then dealing with things dedicated to idolatry (pp. 216–217).

After comparing and contrasting similarities between the *Mishnah*'s responses to these matters alongside Tertullian's decisions on them, Dr. Binder argued that the great church leader "Tertullian lived in close proximity to a Jewish community, founded his arguments on sources that he shared with this community, in the same cultural environment, and reached very similar conclusions."[9] Those interested in her sweep of the aforementioned issues can refer to her monograph. Believing that one illustration will suffice, we will now pick up on a theme noted previously, and consider how both the rabbis and the African church leader Tertullian looked at festivals and sacred space.

The *Mishnah* says, "And these are the festivals of the idolatrous: the *Calends* and the *Saturnalia* and the *Kratesis*" (*Avodah Zarah* 1.3). Archaic as these expressions are, an explanation is warranted at the outset.

"Calends" was used in antiquity to note the first day of a month—and seems to have particularly been used to denote the 1st of January, or the beginning of the Greco-Roman year.[10] "Saturnalia," for its part, was an extremely popular Roman holiday, as well, one held in honor of Saturn

9. Stephanie Binder, "Jewish-Christian Contacts in the Second and Third Centuries, C.E.?" The Case of Carthage; Tertullian and the Mishnah's Views on Idolatry," in Dan Jaffee (ed.), *Studies in Rabbinic Judaism and Early Christianity: Text and Context*, p. 217.
10. Ibid., p. 198.

(or Cronos), the youngest of the Titans and the father of the major gods celebrated by the Greeks and Romans. Foremost among Saturn's sons was the famous Zeus. "Saturnalia," the holiday in his honor, was inaugurated to lift spirits in the wake of a Carthaginian defeat in mid-December. It grew into a weeklong celebration, one accentuated by special foods, clothing, and benefits—with special benefits even extending to slaves. Much as Santa says, "Ho, Ho, Ho," the greeting for the mid- to late-December Saturnalia holiday was "*lo, Saturnalia,*" or "e-o," with "e-o" being a Latin expression similar to Santa's "ho." Lastly, according to Dr. Peter Schafer in *The Talmud Yerushalami and Graeco-Roman Culture, III: Texts and Studies in Ancient Judaism*, the term *Kratesis* was presumed from the rabbinic point of view to describe the founding and beginning of Rome, with Romulus and Remus, and the following ascensions of the ruling emperors. *Kratesis* thus commemorates the beginning of civilization (*natalis urbis*) and as well as, in some sense, the reigning culture's majestic, mythic, and seemingly mystical power.[11] In sum, these holidays celebrate legendary triumphs in Greco-Roman mythology and history.

Avodah Zarah 1.3 put it succinctly and with a warning: "these are the festivals of the idolatrous: the *Calends* and the *Saturnalia* and the *Kratesis.*" So much for the Jews. In his *De Idololatria* 14.4, the church leader Tertullian similarly exhorts North African Christians to avoid "*Saturnalia et calends Ianurias*"—i.e., the mid-December feast to Saturn and the new

11. Peter Schafer (ed.), *The Talmud Yerushalami and Graeco-Roman Culture, III: Texts and Studies in Ancient Judaism*, (Tubingen: J.C.B. Mohr / Siebeck, 2002), p. 342.

year's celebration which comes on its heels.[12]

Associated gift giving was to be shunned by both the Jewish and Christian communities. Tertullian wanted Christians to avoid receiving gifts, as per *De Idololatria* 14.6, much as the Jewish sage Resh Laqish wanted Yehuda the Prince to dispose of a gift received from a *min* (heretic—used at times to refer to Jewish believers in Yeshua) as a New Year's gift, in the *Babylonian Talmud Avodah Zarah* 6B.[13] How ought one to account for the similarity in thinking, here as elsewhere?

Tertullian's familiarity with Judaism may well be attributed to his having once come "near to conversion to Judaism," as some allege.[14] This is no forgone conclusion, however. Dr. Michael Rydelnik, professor of Jewish Studies at the Moody Bible Institute, accepts the idea that Tertullian had not had "any personal knowledge of his opponents and their religion,"[15] i.e., Judaism, an idea he picked up from Williams in *Adversus Judaeos*.[16] (I prefer the notion that he did have personal knowledge.) This discussion aside, that Tertullian's Carthaginian Christians were "found in synagogues" and that they had to be "encouraged to

12. Stephanie Binder, "Jewish-Christian Contacts in the Second and Third Centuries, C.E.?" The Case of Carthage; Tertullian and the Mishnah's Views on Idolatry," in Dan Jaffee (ed.), *Studies in Rabbinic Judaism and Early Christianity: Text and Context*, p. 198.

13. Ibid.

14. Ibid., p. 218.

15. From "The Ongoing Importance of Messianic Prophecy for Jewish Evangelism in the New Millennium," in Darrell L. Bock and Mitch Glaser (eds.) *To the Jew First: The Case for Jewish Evangelism in Scripture and History* (Grand Rapids: Kregel, 2008), p, 273.

16. See also p. 350, n. 47.

preach to Gentiles *too,*" in *De Fuga* 6.2–3,[17] speaks of common ground, natural degrees of familiarity, and mixed associations—something the churchman wanted to weaken and/or break up outright.

Though Tertullian takes on Jews in his *Adversus Iudaeos*, this is but a "stereotyped invention"[18] of Jews—not the real-world Jews of his day. That "he does not attack or evenly openly refer to his Jewish neighbors" in Carthage leads Dr. Binder to argue that he wrote his strident opposition to "prepare Christians for encounters with Jews of the city and wants them to have proper arguments in hand."[19] Spirited disputation is thus not to be construed as being tantamount to disdain. She postulates, "Tertullian [actually] benefited from Jewish associations and inspiration while writing his treatise"—i.e, *De Idolotatria*.[20]

How Tertullian came upon and applied Jewish notions is a matter of conjecture. Did he get them from Jewish believers in Yeshua? Did he get them from his own Jewish associations? We do not know. We do know, though, that Jewish presence and influence is evidenced in Carthage, North Africa.

Dr. Binder's best argument to this effect is that "social, ethnic and religious cosmopolitanism in Carthage [would have] prevented total separation between Jews and Christians"[21]; and, not only that, but the communities could have been so close that "there might [even] have been uncertainty about

17. Italics mine; Ibid., p. 226.
18. Ibid., p. 219.
19. Ibid.
20. Ibid.
21. Ibid., p. 221.

what makes a Christian different from a Jew."[22] "The only definitive conclusion that can be inferred from the study," according to Dr. Binder, "is that when Jewish and Christian communities co-existed in the same place—even though their respective leaders worked hard to maintain a clear theological boundary—on the interpersonal, individual, and social levels, they *were still intertwined and shared their ideas and religious experience*."[23]

Jews and Messianic Jews in Cyrene

Little is known about the birth and spread of the Messianic Jewish movement in Cyrene, North Africa. Here is what we do know, however.

Cyrene was an important Greek colonial city situated in North Africa, midway between Carthage (above) and Alexandria (below). Located on the slopes of the Green Mountains, Cyrene was a short distance from the sea, close to the Greek Peloponnesus and the Greek island called Thera. Part of the Pentapolis, Cyrene was one of the five Greek cities in Libya Cyrenaica (now Tripoli) and was the fourth largest city in the Roman world. Its success was helped by its proximity to the port city Apollonia, which gave it access to international markets.

The Jewish historian Flavius Josephus noted that during the reign of the Ptolemies in Egypt, many Jews took up residency in Cyrene (*Apion* 2.4; *Ant.* 14.7,2; cf. *Targ. Yer.* Gen. x. 13, 14; *Targ.* I Chron. i. 12). In his *The Ancient Memory of Mark: Reassessing Early Church Tradition*, Professor Thomas Oden noted how "refugees of Jewish descent had lived…for three

22. Ibid., p. 222.

23. Italics mine; Ibid., p. 227.

centuries in Cyrene" and that they "consider[ed] themselves as people belonging to the African continent and lodged within its cultures...for well over a millennium before the Arab conquests."[24] They spoke Berber and were called Maghrebim. Along with Hausa and Somali, the Berber language is of afro-asiatic origin and is considered an aboriginal language of North Africa."[25] As evidence of Jewish assimilation, the language was sometimes written with Hebrew letters. Jews who spoke it—along with other languages—extended from Northern Libya to the Saharan oases.

"Some of its Jewish citizens were known to be actively messianic in their hopes and historical perspective," according to Professor Oden, who went on to say that "Messianic Jewish enclaves had been actively present in Cyrenaica."[26] New Testament writers corroborate this assessment, and are keen on noting how some of the prominently placed characters in its pages come from the city of Cyrene—not least of which was John Mark, the author of the first Gospel, known as the Gospel of Mark.

Compelled to carry the cross for Yeshua, Simon was also said to have been a Cyrenian Jew (Matt. 27:32). Luke says Cyrenian Jews were present at Pentecost (Acts 2:10). He went on record further noting how North African Cyrenians even joined with Libertines and formed a Jewish synagogue in Jerusalem (Acts 6:9). Recounting the Gospel's expansion from Judea and to Antioch, Luke then notes in Acts 11 that

24. Thomas C. Oden, *The Ancient Memory of Mark: Reassessing Early Church Tradition* (Downers Grove: IVP Academic, 2011), p. 17.

25. Ibid., p. 19.

26. Ibid.

"some of them were men of Cyprus and Cyrene, which, when they were come to Antioch, spoke unto the Grecians, preaching the Lord Jesus." To this, he added in 13:1 (as noted above), "there were in the church that was at Antioch certain prophets...[among them being a leader named] Lucius of Cyrene."

The New Testament knows Cyrene and establishes various connections, as do Jewish historians. Popular in Jewish history is Jason of Cyrene, whose work is the source of the Second Book of Maccabees, as per *2 Macc.* 2.23. That only minor soundings come from this major city is a source of some disappointment. Those "soundings" tell a story, however.

For their part, Professors Gottheil and Krauss note that, in addition to the city's being made up of seafaring people from Greek lands, "Many [ancient] Jews went from Egypt to Cyrenaica." There, according to Strabo, people "were divided into four classes: citizens, farmers, resident aliens, and Jews." Relegated to the lowest class and thus a much less-than-hoped-for status, Lucullus was once dispatched to Cyrene by Sulla to quell disturbances perpetrated by understandably disenfranchised Hebrews. Concessions to the Jews were recommended by the Romans (*I Macc.* 15. 15–24), and Cyrenians were notified accordingly.

We know that in 74 B.C.E., Cyrene was annexed as a Roman province. According to Josephus, Jewish Cyrenians were then oppressed by the autonomous Greek population (*Ant.* 16. 6.1).[27] Dr. Gottheil and Dr. Krauss explain that the Jews of Cyrene were in close touch with their brethren in Judea and

27. www.newworldencyclopedia.org/entry/Cyrene,_Libya; www.jewishencyclopedia.com/view.

were free to forward their offerings to the Jerusalem Temple (*Ant.* 16.6.5). He said elsewhere that Agrippa sent a letter written in their favor to the Cyrenians (*Wars.* 2.16.4).

Three sons of a certain Ishmael—who was beheaded in Cyrene—were present at the siege of Jerusalem (ib. vi. 2, § 2). After the war ended in Syria, the Romans met with opposition in Cyrene, when the Jewish "Zealot" Jonathan incited the Jews to riot. The disturbance was quickly suppressed by the governor, Catullus (*Wars.* vii. 7.11.1; *Vita,* 76). More serious, according to Professors Gottheil and Krauss, was the insurrection of the Jews of Cyrene under Trajan (117 C.E.), noted above. In conjunction with the overall North African campaign (about which more will be said), the uprising was quelled by Marcius Turbo, but not before about 200,000 Romans and Greeks had been killed (Dio Cassius, lxviii. 32). Wanting to resolve the cascading uprising and ensure that it would not happen again, *the Romans depopulated North Africa of Jews*—and this, of course, included Jewish followers of Yeshua who were well established in the New Testament by their associations with the city.

Though we do not know much about ancient Cyrene regarding the presence of Messianic Jews, we do know that Cyrene was a lively center of Jewish activity and that the New Testament describes various kinds of interactivity with Yeshua-related experience. Were Cyrene not to have fallen prey to anti-Jewish policies, no doubt a strong Messianic Jewish community would have survived and thrived there. It was the birthplace of John Mark, the author of the first Gospel and the individual said by historians in North Africa to have first promoted the Gospel in North Africa after Pentecost.

Jews and Messianic Jews in Alexandria

In "The Jews of Alexandria," Professor Erich Gruen reflects on the experience of better-known Jews in ancient Alexandria, and says:

> Jews [in Alexandria] enjoyed productive and rewarding lives in the greatest of the Hellenistic cities. Integration in the social, economic and cultural life of Alexandria was open to them, and they took advantage of that opening. Jews served in the armies, obtained administrative posts, took part in commerce, shipping, finance, farming and every form of occupation, reaching posts of prestige and importance, and played a role in the world of the Hellenic intelligentsia.[28]

According to Dr. Gruen, Jews fared reasonably well in Egypt. Tragically, however, Jewish communities were destroyed in North Africa. We will now attend to their story, and to their descent from glory to oblivion, while keeping an eye on Messianic Jews.

Successful Egyptian Jews were known to have possessed an independent and lively religious spirit. That, combined with their unyielding monotheistic disposition, their industry, and the social and the political influence they were able to leverage in Egyptian culture by means of it, resulted in a unique and startling Jewish innovation. Over time, successful and independent-

28. Erich S. Gruen, *Diaspora: Jews Amidst Greeks and Romans* (Cambridge: Harvard University Press, 2002), p. 69.

minded Egyptian Jews were able to get social, political, and religious capital working on their behalf, evidenced in part through the manufacture of a magnificent temple in Egypt—one that even rivaled the Temple in Judea. Let us begin our inquiry by considering this little-known marvel.

Dr. Livia Capponi's 2007 work on the temple[29] was reviewed by Professor David Noy of the University of Wales Lampeter for the *Bryn Mawr Classical Review* (2008.09.37). This once-famous (now forgotten) Jewish Temple in Leontopolis, Egypt, was *the only place in Jewish antiquity where sacrifices were offered by Jews outside of Jerusalem.* Most know nothing about this site, nor the story of the Egyptian Jews who built it and frequented it. Before considering Dr. Capponi's work, by way of Dr. Noy's appraisal, a word about the site in question is in order, in part because just introducing the idea of an independent Jewish temple outside Jerusalem may be new to so many readers—as might be the fact that the Jewish population in Egypt was strong enough to leverage it initially and support it thereafter.

Disregarding the confused accountings of the Egyptian temple in the *Talmud*, Dr. Gottheil and Dr. Krauss prefer soundings in Josephus's *Antiquities of the Jews* and *Jewish Wars*, along with Eusebius' *Praeparatio Evangelica.* After noting the Egyptian-based Jewish sanctuary's origination under Onias III's son, who once fled Syrian persecutions and took refuge in Alexandria, Egypt, Josephus says Philometor, King of Egypt, gave him quarter in Egypt. After petitioning him and his sister/wife Cleopatra (not the famous one) to allow

29. In *Il temio di Leontopoli in Egitto: Identita politica e religiosa dei Giudei di Onia. Pubblicazioni della Facolta di Lettere e Filosofia dell'Universita di Pavia.*

him to build a sanctuary in Egypt like the one in Jerusalem, a temple comparable to the one in Jerusalem (though smaller) was built. It was constructed atop the ruins of the temple of Bubastis, in Heliopolis, 180 stadia from Memphis, Egypt.[30] Gottheil and Krauss explain how "Jewish support was crucial in rescuing Julius Caesar at Alexandria, leading him to grant privileges to Jews throughout the Roman Empire."[31] The political influence assisted by providing the necessary political advantage to facilitate the temple's construction.

The Egyptian temple was well known to the writers of the Septuagint, i.e., the Egyptian-manufactured, Greek translation of the Old Testament, known as the LXX. A phrase in Isaiah 19:18, "city of destruction" in Hebrew, was conveniently changed to "city of praise" in the Egyptian-based version, to dovetail with the aforementioned prophecy[32] and enhance the prestige of the then-new Jewish shrine.[33]

These language matters aside, suffice it to note that the rival temple was very well known in Jewish antiquity and was often used by Jews in the region. Interestingly, rabbinic sources seem to neither condone nor condemn it (*Men.* 109a;

---

30. From http://www.jewishencyclopedia.com/view_friendly.jsp?artid=2–6&letter=L.

31. http://bmcr.brynmawr.edu/2008/2008–09–37.html.

32. It is argued that Isaiah had this very temple in mind when he wrote in 19:19–25: "In that day there will be an altar to the Lord in the midst of the land of Egypt, and a pillar to the Lord at its border. And it will be for a sign and for a witness to the Lord of hosts in the land of Egypt….Then the Lord will be known to Egypt, and the Egyptians will know the Lord in that day, and will make sacrifice and offering; yes, they will make a vow to the Lord and perform *it*... the Lord of hosts shall bless, saying, 'Blessed *is* Egypt My people, and Assyria the work of My hands, and Israel My inheritance.'"

33. The NKJV reads: "In that day five cities in the land of Egypt will speak the language of Canaan and swear by the Lord of hosts; one will be called the City of Destruction."

Tosef., Men. xiii. 12–14). Though prominent and well served by the enormous Jewish population in Egypt—which exceeded that in Judea, at the time—Egyptian Jews still dutifully sent sacrifices to the Jerusalem-based Temple. The temple was thus tolerated, based on its enhancing Jewish practices and *not* replacing Jerusalem-based commitments. Whatever ambivalence the rabbis might have had (for understandable reasons), Dr. Capponi argues successfully that the Egyptian temple was "not intended to be schismatic" and was "not [an] attempt to replace Jerusalem as a focus of loyalty," it being "more concerned with introducing greater 'rigor' to Egyptian Judaism" than contributing to its diminution.

"The Jews in Alexandria," according to Professor Gruen, "did not suffer oppression under Ptolemaic or Roman governance; they enjoyed freedom to perform traditional rites and to worship divinity in their own way."[34] So the Egyptian temple served as a gateway—but not a gateway to God. The temple tells a story, and reminds us that Egypt boasted a Jewish population that exceeded Jerusalem's and that Egyptian Jewry supported a temple that rivaled the Herodian Temple in Jerusalem.

It all speaks of magnificence, splendor, and strength. This being so, how can one account for the complete annihilation of Jews in Egypt not long afterward? What happened? Might the event have bearing upon the story of Messianic Judaism in Egypt?

Shortly after the Jerusalem Temple was destroyed in 70 C.E., the Egyptian Temple in Leontopolis was closed by the Roman authorities. "It was closed either by the governor of Egypt, Lupus, or by his successor, Paulinus, about three years

34. Erich S. Gruen, *Diaspora: Jews Amidst Greeks and Romans*, p. 78.

after the destruction of the Temple at Jerusalem." Not only that, we're told, "...the interior furnishings, were confiscated for the treasury of Vespasian, the emperor fearing that through this temple Egypt might become a new center for Jewish rebellion."[35] *The Egyptian temple fell when the Jerusalem Temple was felled.* Much as the Jewish community lived on after the Jerusalem Temple was leveled, so, too, the Jewish community in Egypt lived on after the Egyptian temple's destruction—and the Messianic community, with it—*until the Jewish community in Egypt disappeared after Trajan's revolt of 115–117 C.E.*

In his *Historia Romana* (LXVIII, 32:1–2), the Roman historian Dio Cassius described a Jewish uprising and the consequential utter destruction of North African Jewry—what was referred to as "depopulation" previously. This little-known incident (to most moderns, anyway) had a profound effect on North African Jews—Messianic Jews included.

> ...the Jews in the region of Cyrene [in northern Africa] had put one Andreas at their head and were destroying both the Romans and the Greeks....In all, consequently, two hundred and twenty thousand perished. In Egypt, also, they performed many similar deeds, and in Cyprus under the leadership of Artemio. There, likewise, two hundred and forty thousand perished. *For this reason no Jew may set foot in that land,* but even if one of them is driven upon the island by force of the wind, he is put to death. Various persons took part in subduing these Jews.

35. From http://www.jewishencylopedia.com/view.

In the wake of the horrible ravages of war which left hundreds of thousands dead, Dio says Jews were forbidden to "set foot in the land" of Egypt. This, of course, would include Messianic Jews.

To Dio's story, the following pieces of information may prove helpful.

In 115 C.E., Trajan bested the Parthians in the east, extending western-based Roman hegemony to Armenia, Mesopotamia, and Assyria in the east. Roman troops, which were previously employed to keep the *Pax Romana* (i.e., "Roman Peace") in North Africa, were dispatched to the eastern front for the new Parthian campaign, as a consequence of which North Africa was left less protected. Seething under oppressive Roman racial policies, and unable to get redress for their grievances, seeing an opportunity to throw off the imperial Roman yoke, North African Jews in Cyrene and Cyprus took to arms, and caused no small stir, which invoked the ire of the reigning powers in the process.

As their pent-up furies and enthusiasms were running their course, many non-Jewish people were plundered and the pagan temples of Apollo, Artemis, Hecate, Demeter, Isis, and Pluto were leveled. The death toll was enormous. Gentile refugees fled to Alexandria, Egypt en masse—then, *the largest Jewish population center in the world*—where they exacted their revenge upon the many Jews living there. Two of Alexandria's five districts were Jewish districts, with many Jews living in non-Jewish quarters. The Jewish population in the city alone is said to have been in the vicinity of 150,000 people.

Many were slaughtered.

Not to be outdone, Alexandria's Jews regrouped, after which they spent their furies on even more North African people and places. The temples of Nemesis, Hectate, and Apollo were laid waste. Cyrenaican Jews, as you might recall, similarly marshaled their energies and to destroy the Egyptian countryside. The Roman governor Marcus Rutilius Lupus dispatched the III Cyrenaica and XXII Deiotariana legions to protect the non-Jewish inhabitants of Memphis, Egypt. To these, Trajan then added the Legion VII Claudia, along with forces under Quintus Marcius Turbo, a trusted military man well known to him through his service as prefect of the Praetorian Guard and as the commander of the *Classis Misenensis*, the Roman navy's senior fleet.

Wanting to get a grip on the cascading unrest in North Africa, and needing to ensure the steady flow of Egyptian grain to markets and mouths in Rome, Trajan threw his best at his foes. The able general bested Jewish forts and forces. Myriad Jews in Alexandria and Cyrene were slaughtered, and the campaign was swiftly brought to a close in favor of the Romans.

Wanting to keep the revolt in check and fearing it could well spread from North Africa to the newly acquired, disquieted eastern Syrian-Mesopotamian provinces, Trajan called upon the commander of some North African auxiliaries—a cavalry officer named Lusius Quietus. This capable career officer mobilized his personal and professional resources and imposed himself upon the Jews in Cyprus, Mesopotamia, and Syria—and effectively *annihilated the Jews in the process,* as had Turbo.[36]

36. As a reward for his efficiently effecting the demise of the Jews, Quietus was appointed governor of Judea. Death claimed him in the summer of 118 C.E. Though forgotten by many today, as he lay silently in his grave, Judaism's sages could not keep quiet. They remembered Quietus in the Talmud. There, because of his endeavors to destroy Jewish people and culture, Jewish fathers were exhorted not to teach their sons Greek (*Mishnah Sota,* 9.14).

Quietus thus kept the province quiet.

Truth is, at the moment we know precious little about early Yeshua movement in Egypt and North Africa generally. This is because *the Jewish-based Yeshua movement in Egypt fell prey to the ravages of peoples and circumstances that imposed upon the entire Jewish community—of which they were a part.*

Gone! Just like that. And we know so little.

Given the dearth of Jewish source material, how can one hope to reconstruct aspects of a splinter group within the larger group, i.e., Jewish believers in Yeshua? With Antioch (where our survey began), Alexandria, Egypt was one of the largest cities in the ancient Roman world. It is for this reason that, along with Professor Adolf von Harnack, students of the ancient world forever lament "the most serious gap in our knowledge of primitive church history is our almost total ignorance of the history of Christianity in Alexandria, Egypt."[37] In response to the unsettling absence of materials, Professor Walter Bauer asked in his day—but never successfully answered, "What reason could they have had for being silent about the origins of Christianity in such an important city as Alexandria?"[38]

Since the early Christians were of and among the Jewish people, the absence and silence is due to the fact that Jews in the Alexandrian congregation(s) were annihilated with their

37. Adolf von Harnack, *The Mission and Expansion of Christianity in the First Three Centuries*/2,2 (ET by J. Moffat from the 2nd German edition of 1906; London: Williams and Norgate, 1908); culled from Walter Bauer *Orthodoxy and Heresy in Earliest Christianity* (Tubingen: Siebeck-Mohr, 1964) from http://jewishchristianit.com/Texts/Bauer/bauer02.htm, p. 1.

38. Walter Bauer *Orthodoxy and Heresy in Earliest Christianity* (Tubingen: Siebeck-Mohr, 1964) from http://jewishchristianit.com/Texts/Bauer/bauer02.htm, p. 2.

associated Jewish brethren during the overall Jewish purge. Not content to just say that and leave it, some clues pertaining to Messianic Jewish experience in Egypt can be offered.

Beyond the scant reference in Eusebius of a Jewish revolt under Trajan, a note about Philo and the Therapeutae and Mark, and a succession of ten bishops from Mark to the Emperor Commodus (180-192 c.e.), from Sextus Julius Africanus, Dr. Bauer—with others—wondered what "inexplicable misfortune overtook the [minimal] account of the earliest period of Egyptian church history… [that would] explain the deathly silence."[39] Not wanting to leave the question open, Bauer then leaned upon Professor Karl Muller who said, "It is precisely because of the strength of the Jewish community in Alexandria that Christianity cannot long have been absent from Egypt."[40]

Can we find traces of *early Christian experience* in ancient northern Africa by examining *early Jewish experience*?

Aside from the minimal sources previously noted with Egyptian Jewry specifically, we do have some gnostic Christian voices from Basilides and his son Isidore, Carpocrates and his son Valentinus, Theodotus, Julius Cassianus, and Apelles, a disciple of Marcion. Professor A. M. Nobbs, Director of the Ancient History Research Centre at Macquarie University, Sydney, has worked on a project called "Papyri from the Rise of Christianity in Egypt."[41] A variety of ancient Egyptian documents are

---

39. Ibid.

40. Karl Mueller, *Kirchengeschichte*/2, 1 (Tubingen: Mohr, 1929). Mueller was referenced by Professor Walter Bauer in *Orthodoxy and Heresy in Earliest Christianity* (Tubingen: Siebeck-Mohr, 1964) from http://jewishchristianit.com/Texts/Bauer/bauer02.htm, p. 2, who went on to develop the question and answer, with his work being the principal source for my reflections here, unless otherwise noted.

41. http://www.anchist.mq.edu.au/doccentre/P c.e.overview.htm.

described there, extending to and through the era of Constantine in the early fourth century C.E. Regrettably, the samplings were Spartan and not particularly helpful, except the fact that some, as one from Thebes (perhaps from the fourth century), may possess vestiges of earlier Messianic Jewish origins. The one in question speaks of Abraham, Isaac, and Jesus Christ, together, and refers to "Jesus the *God of the Hebrews*" (Italics mine; PGM IV). That aside, aforementioned gnostic documents, along with Coptic-gnostic gospels (e.g., *Pistis Sophia,* the *Books of Jeu* and the *Gospel of the Egyptians*) constitute the known late first-century and second-century C.E. Christian-like source materials, except the fact that *The Gospel According to the Hebrews* is noted alongside *The Gospel to the Egyptians.*[42] With regard to the *Gospel According to the Hebrews*, Professor Bauer wrote, "If I am not mistaken, the *Gospel of the Hebrews* was the 'Life of Jesus' used by the Jewish Christians of Alexandria." Limited though we indeed are, there are some materials, with one bearing a "heretical trademark" according to Professor Bauer.[43]

"Heretical trademark"!? With so much unsaid, why bother saying that—"heretical"?

Aside from the permeation of gnostic influences, Dr. Bauer notes that Jewish and Gentile believers were "*influenced by the synagogue* with regard to its worship and organization."[44] Interesting, is it not? Need this be problematic?

This "influence" continued until Demetrius, bishop of Alexandria from 189–231 C.E., imposed himself forcefully, and

42. Others have observed the decline of inscriptions associated with pagan, Egyptian architecture, and have seen in this waning enthusiasm for Egyptian paganism an advance of Messianic Judaism's rise.

43. Ibid., pp. 4–5.

44. Italics mine; Ibid., p. 5.

even against the likes of Origen, and then firmly established an episcopal-based, ecclesiastical order more directly under his non-Jewish sway. Since he was not kindly disposed toward Semitic people and structures, one wonders whether Demetrius might have contributed to the "heretical" designation of the ancient Jewish believers in Yeshua and if his disdain can be telling for our purposes?

Bishop Demetrius' lack of appreciation in Semitic lands was described by St. Jerome, who noted that individuals in Palestine, Arabia, Phoenicia, and Achaia did not take him seriously.[45] Believers in the Levant preferred his marginalized interlocutor, Origen. As evidence thereof, in Eusebius' *Ecclesiastical History* 6.2.13–14, a wealthy woman reportedly gave quarter in her household to Origen, along with a famous "heretic" from Alexandria whom she "treated like a son," named Paul. This "son" came originally from Antioch—*the Messianic Jewish base camp.* We are told that "as a consequence of his great reputation, there flocked to him a 'countless host of persons, heretics as well as orthodox believers.'"[46] Thus noted, Eusebius then mentions that St. Ambrose was similarly attracted to Origen and that he, too, was from the Messianic Jewish community in Antioch, as was Paul.

Could it be that Demetrius was unkindly disposed toward Jews and/or Messianic Jewish inclinations? The connections are circumstantial and would prove nothing in a court of law. There is so much that we do not know, and likely cannot know without more to go on. The present scarcity of Egyptian-based

45. Ibid., p. 6.
46. Ibid., p. 7.

source materials leaves the student of early Messianic Jewish history in Egypt frustrated, to be sure. This and other problems notwithstanding, if we cannot find out much about Messianic Jewish experience in Egypt, *can we at least find more on why we cannot find out*?

We can.

Beyond whatever anti-Jewish prejudices may or may not have resonated in the breasts of ancient Egyptian bishops (who aren't here to explain themselves and ward off this author's suspicions about their anti-Jewish dispositions), stepping back and considering early Jewish experience in Egypt, apart from the fledgling church's experience, yields an explanation as to why we don't hear much about Jews in the church. In short, as noted above, *Messianic Judaism died in Egypt when Jewish people and culture were slaughtered there.*

That said, given the openness of Hellenistic Jews and Messianic Jews to non-Jewish individuals, one wonders if and how the movement regrouped and continued on, albeit in non-Jewish dress after the these North African wars.

It seems that, though bested by forces they could not subdue, Torah-based, Yeshua-centered values permeated non-Jewish individuals' hearts and minds in Egypt as elsewhere. As we will see, Torah testimony in a Yeshua context outlived the Jewish community that was completely obliterated in Egypt.

We know this because when a deadly plague utterly ravaged the Roman Empire in the third century C.E., Torah-influenced Yeshua believers of the next generation rose to the occasion and garnered the affections of many non-believers in the process. To the previous accountings, the following Alexandrian-based story is worth adding. Writing at the height of the second great epidemic in 260 C.E., Bishop Dionysius of Alexandria said:

> Most of our brother Christians showed unbounded love and loyalty, never sparing themselves and thinking only of one another. Heedless to danger, they took charge of the sick, attending to their every need and ministering to them in Christ, and with them departed this life serenely happy; for they were infected by others with the disease, drawing on themselves the sickness of their neighbors and cheerfully accepting their pains. Many, in nursing and curing others, transferred their deaths to themselves and died in their stead.... The best of our brothers lost their lives in this manner, a number of presbyters and deacons and laymen winning high commendation so that death in this form, the result of great piety and strong faith, seems in every way the equal of martyrdom.[47]

That sort of activity was similarly confirmed by Cyprian, the ancient and famous Bishop of Carthage in 251 C.E., when he described Christian conduct during the horrific plague in *Morality* 15–20:

> [T]he just are dying with the unjust... How suitable, how necessary it is that this plague and

47. Culled from Rodney Stark, *The Rise of Christianity: A Sociologist Reconsiders History,* p. 81.

> pestilence, which seems horrible and deadly, searches out the justice of each and every one and examines the minds of the human race; whether they well care for the sick, whether relatives dutifully love their kinsmen as they should, whether masters show compassion for their ailing slaves, whether physicians do not desert the afflicted.[48]

In his *Apology* 39, Tertullian of Carthage noted, "It is our care of the helpless, our practice of loving kindness that brands us in the eyes of many of our opponents. 'Only look,' they say, 'look how they love one another.'"[49] This premium on hospitality derives from Jewish sources.

Torah-based, Messianic Jewish communities were organized like Jewish synagogues precisely in such a way as to deliver on this stellar Jewish virtue. Being kindly disposed toward disenfranchised aliens, tending to the sick, and administrating this benevolence through deacons and presbyters were well established, synagogue-based Jewish activities. When, for example, Paul instructed Timothy in 1 Tim. 3:1–13 to find worthy bishops and deacons who were blameless, connected to one marriage partner, not given to vice but inclined toward virtue, able family administrators and the like, he was borrowing from pre-existing lists of virtues employed in the synagogue to describe requirements for leaders who were vested with juridical authorization and empowered to distribute monies to those in need.

48. Ibid., p. 81.
49. Ibid., p. 87.

Yale's Professor Abraham Malherbe explains:

> The stock-in-trade of the Greek moralists—for example the lists of vices and virtues, the moral commonplaces, the oratory styles—are all found in Paul and other New Testament writings… Instruction on how to behave toward the gods, the state, married partners and to children assumed a recognizable form. Such lists appear in Hellenistic Jewish and Christian writings.[50]

Speaking of "lists," Dr. Malherbe's observation is best considered alongside that of the late Dr. Alfred Edersheim, who sheds light on the Christian employment of Jewish benevolence-related structures in his classic *Sketches of Jewish Social Life in the Days of Christ*:

> The special qualification for the office of Sanhedrinist, mentioned in the Rabbinical writings, are such as to remind us of the directions of St. Paul to Timothy (1 Tim. 3:1–10). [To this, remember what the Talmud says, that a] member of the Sanhedrin must be wise, modest, God-fearing, truthful, not greedy for filthy lucre, kindly, not a gambler, nor a usurer (*Sanh*. iii. 3).[51]

50. Abraham Malherbe, *Social Aspects of Early Christianity* (Philadelphia: Fortress Press, 1983), pp. 50-51.

51. Alfred Edersheim, *Sketches of Jewish Social Life in the Days of Christ* (Grand Rapids: Eerdmans, 1982), p. 282.

Not "greedy for money" is noted, is it not? Listed are character requirements. The connection between the Jewish and Messianic Jewish (or Christian) offices, practices, and virtues are telling—as is the lack of such virtue in pagan antiquity. In order to round off the point and demonstrate that Paul was using the same list of virtues, it is worth noting the words of the city's most famous Jew, Philo:

> None such is a disciple of the holy word (i.e., Logos) but only those who are really men, enamored of moderation, propriety and self-respect: men who have laid down as a foundation, so to speak, of their whole life self control, abstemiousness, endurance, which are safe road-steads of the soul, in which they can lie firmly moored and out of danger; men superior to the temptations of money, pleasure [and] popularity.

To sum it up, *virtue-rich caring and sharing were part and parcel to what it meant to be religious—in a Jewish sense*, anyway, and a Messianic Jewish one by spiritual relation and social association. This value was lost to the pagans, whose gods were not the least bit known to be loving toward humankind and only minimally interested in human affairs in the first place.

This is described by Dionysius, who showed how the heathen tough got going when the going got tough in the days of the dreaded plague:

> The heathen performed in the opposite way. At the first onset of the disease, they pushed the sufferers away and fled from their dearest, throwing them into the roads before they were dead and treated unburied corpses as dirt, hoping thereby to avert the spread and contagion of the fatal disease; but do what they might, they found it difficult to escape.[52]

This simply was not the Jewish way, nor the Messianic Jewish way, to be sure.

Though circumstantial, it could be argued that Messianic Judaism—or early Christianity—survived its scourges and purges in Egypt and lived on in the Empire. Though many have lost sight of the Jewish origins of what has been called the Christian faith and virtue, its anchor in Jewish soil is simply undeniable.

52. Ibid., p. 82.

CONCLUSION

So, what might one gather from this assessment of ancient Messianic Jewish experience, if anything?

We need a revolution in our thinking—not just an evolution.

The Christian story is inextricably bound to the Jewish story. While Christianity represents something of an evolution, to be sure, a revolution is in order—both to transform the interrelationships that impose themselves upon us so radically and to force a reorientation of our thinking.

What we think we see in the canonical New Testament and non-canonical sources is something we must decide for ourselves. For this writer, the notion that Messianic Judaism morphed into a *non*-Jewish Christian religion under Paul's influence is called into question in both the New Testament itself and in post-New Testament literature. Though this idea of a non-Jewish Pauline Christianity has held for many hundreds of years, it is simply not substantiated in the primary sources. In the New Testament, one is hard-pressed to find a *non*-Jewish Paul or an *anti*-Jewish Christianity—period.

A more careful assessment of the sources argues that early Christianity, so called, should be construed as a more liberal and more global extension of Jewish vision and practice. It is a natural outgrowth of Jewish religious experience. Though frequently portrayed as Christianity's vanquished rival, Judaism holds a much more pivotal place in the story.

Speaking of "vanquished," another notion is called into question here—that the demise of the Jerusalem Temple was a historical turning point, a theological turning point, and a Providential sign that God was finished with recalcitrant Jews. Though many claim this event as proof that God abandoned the Jewish people and freed himself to work on a growing Christian church, the destruction of the Temple in 70 c.e. should not be construed as anything of the sort. That Messianic Judaism survived and thrived in Jerusalem long after the Temple's demise is directly confirmed in all the literature, offering proof of God's abiding presence with the people and the place.

Messianic Judaism's profound impact on classical "Christian" literature in and around the Mediterranean world after the Temple's destruction is also corroborated by these primary sources, highlighting Messianic Judaism's strength in a new and increasingly non-Jewish economy even long after Messianic Jews were driven from their ancestral homeland. Christianity, so called, began within a completely Jewish framework and continued to be Jewish for many years despite claims to the contrary.

My engagement with both the sources themselves and with scholars more able than myself who reflected on the sources and offered superior commentary had the net effect of instilling a profound sense of humility in me, mindful as I am of how much I don't know about ancient Jewish/Christian origins and likely will never know. My hope is that younger scholars will pursue some of these findings and discover a deeper revelation of the way we once were, one that will shed important light on the past and future of all the people of God. This would give me great pleasure indeed.

Speaking of pleasure, let me thank you for going on the journey around the Mediterranean world with me and for graciously bearing any understatements, overstatements, or mistakes of fact in these pages. Your interest in who the first followers of Yeshua really were, and what Messianic Jewish experience really was, lends credence to the proposition that you are a modern extension of the ancient people described in this volume. I am thrilled that you exist, that we exist, and that we are experiencing a resurgence of Messianic Jewish faith and practice—truly a miracle in our times.

About the Author

Jeffrey Seif was born and raised in Jewish home. After coming to faith in Yeshua and after experiencing a subsequent calling into ministry, Jeff went to prepare at the Moody Bible Institute, in Chicago, and finished with both a master's degree and doctorate from Southern Methodist University, Dallas. Dr. Seif has authored many books, but is best known for his years leading the nationally syndicated television program entitled "Zola Levitt Presents." He has served as a Bible college and seminary professor for twenty-three years. Professor Seif is also a proud graduate of the North Texas Regional Police Academy, has a career in Law Enforcement, and currently serves as a Reserve Officer in the Dallas area, working sixteen hours per month. Dr. Seif is also the rabbi of Prince of Peace / Sar Shalom Congregation in the Dallas-area. He can be reached through drjeffreyseif.com.

COMPLETE JEWISH BIBLE
The Lives and Ministries of ELIJAH and ELISHA
Dr. Walter C. Kaiser, Jr.
Dear You Letters of Identity in Yeshua for Women
PRAYING LIKE the JEW, JESUS
JONES
Van der Meulen & Malda
His Names Are Wonderful
Barbara D. Malda
Come and Worship
Under THE FIG TREE
תחת התאנה
PATRICK GABRIEL LUMBROSO
פטריק גבריאל לומברוזו
Under THE VINE
תחת הגפן
PATRICK GABRIEL LUMBROSO
פטריק גבריאל לומברוזו
Making Eye Contact with God
GILLESPIE
You Bring the Bagels, I'll Bring the Gospel
RUBIN
THE WORLD TO COME
LEMAN
Psalms & Proverbs
David H. Stern
MESSIANIC JUDAISM
STERN
RESTORING THE JEWISHNESS OF THE GOSPEL
STERN
GOD'S APPOINTED CUSTOMS
KASDAN
GOD'S APPOINTED TIMES
KASDAN
Passover:
GATEWAYS TO TORAH
RABBI RUSSELL RESNIK
CREATION to COMPLETION
RESNIK
Is Christ Really THE END of THE LAW?
The Red Heifer
To the Ends of the Earth
Dr. Jeffrey L. Seif
On The Way to Emmaus
Dr. Jacques Doukhan
THEY LOVED THE TORAH
Friedman
YESHUA
A Guide to the Real Jesus and the Original Church
MOSELEY
CONVEYING A HERITAGE
JEWISH NEW TESTAMENT COMMENTARY
MATTHEW PRESENTS YESHUA, KING MESSIAH
KASDAN
PHILIPPIANS
R. SEAN EMSLIE
LUMBROSO

Printed in the United States
by Baker & Taylor Publisher Services